RADICAL
SIMPLICITY

RADICAL SIMPLICITY

How simplicity transformed a
loss-making mega brand into
a world-class performer

KEN ALLEN

EBURY
PRESS

1 3 5 7 9 10 8 6 4 2

Published in 2019 by Ebury Press, an imprint of Ebury Publishing,
20 Vauxhall Bridge Road,
London SW1V 2SA

Ebury Press is part of the Penguin Random House group of companies
whose addresses can be found at global.penguinrandomhouse.com

Text © Ken Allen 2019

First published by Ebury Press in 2019

www.penguin.co.uk

A CIP catalogue record for this book is available from the British Library

ISBN 9781529104721

Typeset in 11/16.5 pt Garamond MT Std
by Integra Software Services Pvt. Ltd, Pondicherry

Printed and bound in Great Britain by Clays Ltd, Elcograf S.p.A.

Penguin Random House is committed to a sustainable future for
our business, our readers and our planet. This book is made
from Forest Stewardship Council® certified paper.

To my friends and family, especially my wife Gigi, without whose support this book wouldn't have been possible and who have been so accepting of my constant preoccupation with getting it finished. I dedicate it to my beloved children, Lisa, Danielle, Nicole and Alexander. 'You are the sons and daughters of life's longing for itself.' (Taken from *The Prophet*, by kahlil Gibran, Knopf 1923). I simply wish you long, healthy and happy futures.

CONTENTS

PREFACE:
DHL, THE MATURE DISRUPTOR

Every day, a little miracle happens, some one million times. Someone, who could be anywhere in the world, from Manila to Manchester or from Bhutan to Bolivia, will receive a package. It could contain an item of clothing they've been eagerly awaiting – something they've purchased on the Internet, perhaps. Or it could contain a replacement part for a machine their business relies on that is running worryingly close to breaking point. Whether they are delighted, relieved, impressed or disappointed with their purchase, they will probably spare little thought for the delivery driver whose touchscreen they scribbled their signature on when they took delivery of the package. And they will spare even less thought for the sorting centre operators, the airside workers, the customs brokers or the service centre leaders who worked together all over the world, in order to ensure that their purchase arrived at its destination on time.

In 1969, two monumental events took place. The first was that man walked on the moon for the first time, fulfilling the goal that JFK had set in 1962 – the famous 'one small step for man, one giant leap for mankind'. The second event was the establishment of DHL in San Francisco – and this was another major step that would shrink the world.

DHL was a true pioneer in a new industry that became known as international express delivery. The company was a classic start-up: it might have had limited funds, but it was massively entrepreneurial, fast-growing, extremely customer-focused and had a truly committed workforce. Unfortunately however, it struggled to be profitable, to the extent that in 2002, 33 years after the company had been founded, it was losing over €150 million a year. Despite this, it was a strong global brand, a fact that led to its acquisition by Deutsche Post.

In 2008, with the global financial crisis on the horizon, the company, which was by then almost 40 years old, was almost bankrupt, having accumulated losses of €2.2 billion in that year. In 2009, Ken Allen, then a veteran of the Express part of the business who had been working at the company for 24 years, was promoted to the position of global CEO. Over the next ten years, Ken and his team achieved one of the greatest turnarounds in the history of the transport and logistics industry. They adopted a simple, people-based approach to the business by focusing on motivating their staff to deliver great service quality, which resulted in loyal customers and a profitable network. Express is now the best-performing division in the Deutsche Post DHL Group: it generated earnings in excess of €1.9 billion in 2018 (with a 12 per cent margin) and was voted the sixth best place in the world to work by *Fortune* magazine.

Sometimes known as 'the Singing CEO', Ken is enthusiastic about emphasising the simple things that bring people together and help get the message across to everyone in the organisation: music, sport, love and logistics. Put simply, he wants everyone who works at DHL to be an ambassador for the brand: he believes everyone is a salesperson and wants them to be so enthusiastic that at the start of a working week, they shout, 'Yes – it's Monday morning and I'm back to work at DHL!'

This book will highlight the need for the sort of human leadership that delivers a simple message about how everyone can contribute and be a superstar for their company, whether big or small. And it will also show how Ken and his team built an 'Insanely Customer-centric Culture' and how they get so upset at the thought of disappointing a customer that they feel sick to the stomach.

The ideas that Ken introduced were radically simple – to focus on the core, build the greatest international express company on the planet and certify every employee as a specialist. It was his skill at executing the ideas that transformed them from a mere vision into a reality.

In 2019, DHL turns 50 years old, which is actually quite old in business terms. We hear a lot now about 'disruption' and the threats and opportunities brought about by digitalisation and having increased access to low-cost capital. DHL was a classic disruptor of an earlier age, because they saw the incredible opportunity provided by the globalisation that began during the late 1960s. Companies accelerated their presence in foreign markets at a rapid rate as trade policies were liberalised and improved aviation networks shrank the world.

The traditional method of moving documents around the world was the postal service, but airmail was both slow and unreliable; shipping companies and banks needed a faster and more reliable service that would help drive efficiency for their customers. In true entrepreneurial style, with limited capital and in direct competition with the established national postal services, the company's founders opened up in 125 countries, with over 700 stations in the first 15 years.

In the seventies and eighties, the era of 'time-based competition' kicked in. Companies globally looked for shorter lead times as lower stock levels and just-in-time (JIT) manufacturing became the norm. A combination of this new sort of manufacturing with the growth of consumerism and the logistics revolution saw global trade growing at four to five times the rate of GDP. DHL was perfectly positioned to take advantage of this tremendous opportunity, and during the 1990s it grew by something close to 1,500 per cent.

Today, DHL is helping new disruptors to acquire a global presence incredibly quickly. Small and medium-sized enterprises, as well as large corporations, can all use the company's integrated global network to distribute products instantly anywhere in the world. In this age of online e-commerce and global payment systems, many of us are global citizens and make the most of the opportunity to travel the world through low-cost airlines – the world is now one homogeneous market. This is the idea that is at the heart of the strength of DHL – the most international company in the world is always ready to help young disruptors become global.

As a mature disruptor, Ken sees his role as keeping on reinforcing simple messages: focus on the core, motivate the staff to deliver great service quality, maintain customer loyalty and deliver a profit for shareholders. This is, after all, why he decided to give this book the title *Radical Simplicity* – as you'll learn from reading it, there is nothing common about common sense.

INTRODUCING THE DHL TURNAROUND

DHL Express has delivered one of the biggest turnarounds in the history of transportation.

Jeff Ward, A.T. Kearney, Global Management Consulting

A.T. Kearney is a global management consulting firm with offices in 40 countries around the world. Jeff Ward is a consultant with the business based in Chicago who has more than 20 years' experience working with clients in the freight transport and logistics industry. The following is an extract from his report on the turnaround of DHL Express written in 2017.

Ken Allen delivered one of the biggest turnarounds in transportation industry history. This was the most impactful, quickest transformation that I have ever witnessed. DHL Express went from the worst to the best performing company among its competitors and within the Deutsche Post DHL portfolio. The financial results, market share gain and service performance were outstanding. It's a real accomplishment to even manage a company with the size and reach of DHL Express, let alone turn it around.

Ken focused the entire company on the single mission of being the premier international express company. That required the company to exit many

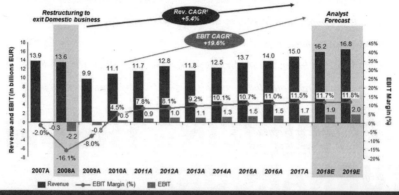

DHL Express has delivered one of the biggest turnarounds in the history or transportation

Results and Analyst Expectations for DHL Express

How can DHL Express maintain its momentum in a changing world?

1. Revenue CAGR of +5.4% for period of 2009-2017. EBIT CAGR of +19.6% for period 2010-2017.
Source: Stifel, Nicolaus & Company analyst report, A.T. Kearney

A.T. Kearney XX/ID   1

domestic markets, but also raised the average revenue to the price points attached to international service. The higher yields drove higher earnings that enabled investments in the business, such as new planes and sorting facilities. It was a bold move and required a leap of faith. But Ken deftly and quickly led the company through the transformation. And the rapid success gave the organisation confidence that they could maintain the earnings momentum and deal with the next horizon of challenges, like the growth in B2C and heavier shipment weights.

The decentralised structure of DHL, which one might think a hinderance to a rapid turnaround, was rather an enabler because of the culture of accountability and innovation. The creativity and commitment of the executive team was amazing. Ken and his team kept raising the bar in healthy increments and the organisation responded. DHL Express quickly developed a cadence of consistent sustainable growth and improvement.

The size and culture of a large corporation like Deutsche Post might also seem to have been a hinderance. And of course there are some natural conflicts between a large corporation and a fast-moving express company in the middle of a transformation. But Ken and Frank Appel have an excellent relationship *and they complement each other in important ways that were key to the success. Frank gave Ken the support and latitude inside Deutsche Post DHL that was required to make the turnaround possible.*

In retrospect, it all seems so simple. The international express business is already so complex and in so many countries. Why add the complexity of so many different domestic products and price points? But this gets at the heart of Ken Allen as a leader. He sees problems clearly and acts decisively. Ken made the tough calls, the right calls that changed everything. Plus he was the right person, at the right time, in the right position. He is a global citizen and comfortable with any culture or people around the world. And he had deep roots in the legacy of DHL that helped him lead the company back to its roots and focused on a great future.

Jeff Ward, A.T. Kearney, Global Management Consulting

INTRODUCTION:
SIMPLICITY, THE FORGOTTEN DISCIPLINE

Bob Seger is an American singer-songwriter. I've never met him, but if I ever do, I'll tell him he expressed the essence of who I am and what I believe. 'Simplicity' is a word that articulates many of my favourite things: the idea of something being of humble origins, free of ostentation, uncomplicated, unrestricted, understandable, actionable and of having one main cause. In a nutshell, to me it means having the freedom and peace of mind to do *what* matters most *when* it matters most. When I keep things simple, I am able to make friends and influence people: I make others happy, and they feel in control because I help protect them against distraction and feeling overwhelmed.

When I decided to write this book, people told me that deciding on a title would be one of the most difficult parts of the process. Actually, I found it relatively straightforward – simple, in fact. And in many ways, that sums up my perspective on success in business. Keep it simple. What I call 'Radical Simplicity' is taking all the established wisdom and being almost manic in its execution. I will outline a framework called SELF Reflection that makes the concept so much more concise. In essence, it's all about stripping away anything that interferes with the things that matter, about guarding against the creep of bureaucracy, the lure of vanity and the avoidance of responsibility. It's about making sure that all our efforts serve our customers in a way that grows our business profitably. If I cannot say something simply, I know I probably don't understand it. And I know for sure that I can understand it when I'm able to explain to others what I mean in a way they can easily understand. I've loved my time working at DHL; I love what we've achieved and the difference we've made. And over the past 35 years I've discovered some simple rules for success, which I'm excited to share with you here.

I am a simple man in a complex world, but that doesn't mean I'm stupid or slow. In fact, it means I am able to WIN by focusing on What's Important Now. I look for the things that matter and invest my time in making them better – I simply have no time for anything else.

In the 50 years that I've been working, I've progressed from being a humble accounts clerk to a global CEO. DHL Express, the company I have had the privilege to run, is also turning 50 in 2019. So this is my simple story – and at its heart is a massively successful business turnaround, which was achieved mainly as a result of an emphasis on simplicity – radically applied. It's also the story of a mature disruptor who has come of age and has some lessons to share. It's a simple story, and some of what you read may well be blindingly obvious, because a lot of what we do in business seems to be common sense. But as my father always tells me, 'There is nothing common about common sense. Just as there is nothing basic about the basics.'

My journey charts what can happen when you make Radical Simplicity part of your daily practice. I hope you find it useful, practical and entertaining – and if you change just one thing about the way you run your business as a result of reading this, then this book will have done its job.

CHAPTER 1:
A YORKSHIREMAN'S GUIDE TO STRATEGY
(AND YOU CAN'T GET MUCH SIMPLER THAN THAT)

Being a global CEO can often feel a bit like being a gardener in a cemetery –
there are a lot of people underneath you, but none of them are listening!

My turnaround at DHL Express has been due to a large extent to 100,000 people around the globe all choosing to listen and deciding to play their individual parts in delivering our Focus strategy – it's as simple as that. If I had not had such a receptive workforce, I doubt I would be writing this book. That begs the question – why do so many companies find it so difficult to connect the people in their organisation with their strategy and goals? And why are they unable to help them see what part they could play in creating a successful business with a prosperous future?

Is it to do with the content of the strategy or its delivery, or is it a combination of both? I have found the following thoughts relating to the introduction of a new strategy helpful during my career:

- If it is too complex for the audience to understand easily, no one will listen.
- If it changes every six months or each year, no one will listen.

- If it is boring, no one will listen.
- If you can't explain it simply, you don't understand it well enough yourself and no one will listen.

I realise that this all sounds like common sense, but I have seen enough over-complicated, mind-numbingly boring and constantly changing strategies over the years and have also spent a lot of time thinking about why strategies often fail to deliver the positive results that they promise. So think of this as a Yorkshireman's guide to strategy. You can't get much simpler than that!

I prize simplicity, but I also recognise that the business world is filled with complexity, among which there is:

- Unpredictable external economic and political factors.
- Emerging competitors, who can be disruptive.
- Changing customer preferences and expectations.
- Technology and digitalisation, which can mean a stream of new opportunities.
- Complex networks of interest groups.
- An ever-changing workforce.

All these factors can be overwhelming and tough to navigate, but I've always thought that we can make a business much more manageable if we look at it through the lens of SELF Reflection (for more on this, see pages 18–19):

SIMPLICITY

We all crave simplicity and know it makes sense in business, so when it comes to crafting strategy why is it forgotten – and how does complexity creep in?

1) Companies don't believe they are able to gain a strategic advantage through a reliance on simple ideas – this is the idea that if something was that easy, everyone would already be doing it.
2) Many strategies are written by external analysts or consultants, and nobody wants to pay for simple advice. As a result, complicated language

is often used to disguise things that are, in fact, simple and blindingly obvious.

3) Many organisations have a set-up that is strictly functional and not reflective of their process or customer journey – so strategy ends up as a patchwork of silo thinking, with plans that aren't properly joined up.

4) Companies don't often use strategy to align everything they do and get swamped with too many different things, causing them to lose focus.

5) Many organisations fail to ask the killer questions – such as 'How does this strategy translate to the front line, and how do we make it operational?'

If we thought and acted differently, we would see that there are huge benefits in keeping strategy both simple to understand and execute. Any intelligent fool can make things bigger and more complex, but it takes a touch of genius and a lot of courage to move in the opposite direction.

The discipline of Radical Simplicity means rejecting the things that don't develop our core offering and that distract us from focusing on executing our strategy. This requires strong leadership to stand up and resist diversionary activity. It's time to create not-to-do lists rather than to-do lists.

They say that it takes a year for strategic messages to be embedded throughout the entirety of each level of an organisation, which means that in most companies it could take five years or more to reach all levels of the organisation. So consistency and simplicity are key to make sure front-line employees know what is expected and how they can get involved. So my message is that a great strategy is a simple one, as well as one that appeals to the whole organisation and is understood by every front-line employee. It can also be implemented by everyone in an organisation, and quickly!

EXECUTION

Is writing a simple strategy, built round a core unique and compelling competence the whole story? No it's not. Eighty-six per cent of strategies look the same and are so hard to tell apart that they morph into one homogenous mass. They all herald the importance of winning customers' preference, increasing profitability and market share and growing a happy and productive workforce, as well as the number of happy investors. They all look and sound as good as each other. What sets good and poor strategies apart from each other isn't the uniqueness or the quality of how they are expressed – it's the execution of them that is the key differentiator. Even when the strategy is simple and based on sound research and rigorous thinking, the key challenge is finding people who have the ability to execute effectively and get the job done. If 90 per cent of strategy is execution, 90 per cent of execution is based on people. And if it is all about people, they need leadership and they need focus.

LEADERSHIP

When I look at various businesses, I often see a myriad of people who joined them at very senior levels from other companies. Many of them try admirably to implement strategies that were relevant in their previous worlds, but they frequently find that what's worked in their previous worlds doesn't easily translate into their new ones. It's not that they are bad leaders, but they don't recognise the complexities of their new operating systems and cultures. And as a result, their strategies are not widely understood by the people who have to execute them and they are not effectively implemented, stunting profitability and demotivating people. My advice is as follows:

1) There is only one strategist, and that is the CEO. Everyone else can have their own input, of course, but the CEO is ultimately responsible. If the strategy works the CEO stays, but if it fails, it's time to speed-dial the headhunter!

2) Focus on what you are world-class at, not on trying to fix what you are not good at.

3) Be brave – publish your strategy, including financials, in a document that is visible and understandable to the whole organisation. This will force you to lay everything out in terms that any employee can read and understand and act on.

4) Focus on execution – once you have a strategy, everyone's priority should be getting it done. In just about every case relating to the execution of strategy or complex projects, the critical question is 'Who?' Who in our organisation has the experience, track record and capability to get the job done? Leaders have to be experts.

FOCUS

The most successful strategies are based on a few simple rules:

1. A business has to make money before it can do anything else

Always start by focusing on the basics. Being profitable is what really matters as a foundation to build something incredible. As the legendary management consultant and author Peter Drucker says, 'Results are the only true sign of excellence.'

I have been involved in a number of turnarounds. You have to cut costs quickly and deeply to obtain a profitable cost position, leave the peripheral businesses you are not good at and focus on the core. A focus on financial results and profitability are not just for turnarounds – in my view, the real heroes are the CEOs who manage to grow their revenue and profit consistently year after year. They make money and they invest wisely – it's a tough balancing act, but it gives them the licence to develop and grow their businesses over the long term.

2. The only way to long-term profitability is through satisfied and loyal customers

The aim of a business is to create and keep a customer and the ability to grow, be profitable, invest and develop new capabilities, and all this is driven by customer loyalty. In fact, if you really want to be successful, you'll need to do what we've done at DHL and build an 'Insanely Customer-centric Culture'. Loyal customers are your best advertisement and the surest route to profitability, so get out there, listen to them and act on what they tell you. When I travel around and do town-hall events with DHL staff, I often ask 'Who here is in Sales?' and repeat the question until everyone's hands are in the air. It's another one of my simple beliefs – everyone has to be a salesperson. If you're not out meeting your customers, how can you know and manage your business?

3. Great service quality justifies a price premium

Customers' loyalty is driven by competitive prices and great products and service. If you can genuinely deliver great service quality that sets you apart from the competition, you will be able to charge a premium, and that's what gives you superior returns. In turn, it's these returns that allow you to invest in brand-building, systems and staff.

4. Loyal customers and great service quality are the results of highly motivated people

Teams of employees who are exceptionally well trained and have access to great systems and tools are the ones who tend to go the extra mile. More crucially they understand the critical long-term importance of retaining customers. Motivated people follow processes and they know that in order to give the customer the service quality they demand, they need to do everything by the book – if everyone follows a standard operating procedure to the letter, then the product or service will be delivered on time, every time. Furthermore, motivated people also have huge empathy for the customer, so in those cases where things do go wrong, they are able to take ownership and work diligently to fix the problem.

5. Once you are enjoying profitable growth, you need to strengthen your commitment to your people

A great culture can be the ultimate source of competitive advantage and the start of a virtuous circle, whereby motivated people drive great service quality, which results in loyal customers who are the drivers of a profitable business. Put simply, success in business starts and ends with happy people. If you genuinely want to motivate, you have to have an affinity with your staff, especially those on the front line. In many instances, they are in front of customers every day and so it is critical that they are able to communicate the key messages – the best way to do that is through having a clear, concise, simple strategy.

REFLECTION

My biggest reflection on how to win in strategy is 'Don't worry about competitors – worry about customers.' If you concentrate completely on getting things right for them, the competition will cease to be a threat. That's what my Focus strategy was built to do. It has all the same things that most great and simple strategies have, but I also tried to tap into the things that bring us together as humans – music, sport, love and logistics.

The success of my strategy is all about how we can take the things that bring us together and make them relevant to everybody. If people are having fun, they bring a lot more of themselves to their work. A smile and a laugh are often enough to differentiate us from our competitors if they are going about their work without any of our *joie de vivre*. After all, a smile says the same thing in every language.

KEY LEARNING

- There is nothing basic about the basics.
- If it isn't a clear yes, then it's a clear no.
- Ninety per cent of strategy is execution. Ninety per cent of execution is people.
- There is only one strategist – the CEO.
- Focus on what you are world class at.
- Be brave. Publish your strategy, including financials.
- The only way to long-term profitability is satisfied customers.
- Great service and products are the results of highly motivated people.
- Don't worry about competitors, worry about customers.

CHAPTER 2:
IT'S NOT ABOUT WHO'S RIGHT
IT'S ABOUT WHO'S LEFT

A prosecutor stood up in a courtroom and presented his case to the judge, who
  looked at him and said, 'You are absolutely right.'
Then the defence stood up and presented his case. The judge looked at him and
  said, 'You are absolutely right.'
Both men turned to the judge and said, 'We can't both be absolutely right.'
  The judge looked back at them and said, 'You are absolutely right.'

The moral of the story is that just being right won't win you the case. That's just step one; after that you have to keep your focus, faith and fitness to stay the distance. The person who will be successful is the one who is still standing at the end of a long and gruelling contest.

In 1985, I joined DHL Express as a Finance Manager in the Middle East; today, I am its global CEO. I am also a board member of Deutsche Post, the owner of DHL and one of the biggest companies in the world, which has an annual revenue of €65 billion. I have rung the closing bell on Wall Street, shaken hands with the pope, consulted with the prime minister of France, been a founding partner of Formula E, appeared in *GQ* magazine dressed in Vetements fashion, presented a trophy to Lewis Hamilton at a Formula 1 race, sponsored the Rugby World Cup and even spent time with Manchester United greats.

I'm not saying all this to impress you; on the contrary, I'm telling you because I'm amazed that any of it has happened to me. My story is the unlikely tale of a coal miner's son who inadvertently discovered the secret of success and was smart enough to recognise it. Henry Kissinger once said, 'A diamond is a chunk of coal that did well under pressure', and I think that's a description that describes me perfectly. I am living proof that we can get better as we get older. I want my last year to be my best year, my last day to be my best day. Simply put: Best Day Every Day.

I was born at home on 2 August 1955 in Horbury, a small town of around ten thousand people in West Yorkshire. I grew up on a council estate, the eldest of six children – by the time I turned ten, I had two brothers and three sisters. My mother was a nurse and my father worked as a coal miner. I don't think he ever really liked what he did for a job, but it was the thing that paid the most for the skills that he had. He retired after the miners' strike in the 1980s when he was only 53, and never regretted it for a moment. In a way, he was the opposite of a role model for me – I never want to do something I don't enjoy. We might not have had much, but I certainly didn't want for anything and I have no unhappy memories of those early years. We didn't have any spare time or money for things that weren't necessary, and I often think that this informs my business philosophy even now, over 50 years later. Even though I now lead the most international company in the world, I think it is clear that my Yorkshire roots have defined my approach to leadership and management. As we say in Yorkshire: you should 'like what you say, and say what you bloody well like'.

In primary school, although I was naturally bright, I never learned to study effectively and when it came to exams, I would often resort to just cramming the night before. I didn't go to university because I didn't enjoy academic study – I found it all rather boring, and yearned instead for some experience of the real world. When I was 16, having left school, I started my first job at the famous Slazenger factory in Horbury, where the footballs for the 1966 World Cup were made. I worked in the accounts department, and the company's management seemed to see something in me that I couldn't at that stage see in myself. They guided me onto a career path that I would not have found on my own, encouraging me to become an accountant. None of my friends at the time were ambitious, and some of them were pretty rough. While I didn't have a specific professional goal, I knew I had to get ahead of the people with whom I was associating – I knew even then that you become the company you keep; by that measure, I worried that I wasn't going to become anything.

When I was 19, my girlfriend got pregnant and my beautiful first daughter, Lisa, was born. Being a 'family man' actually provided me with the stability to work and study. It also positioned me as a more mature person at work. The responsibility of being a husband and a father made me more determined to become a decent provider so I was able to support my family.

Changing direction in my life was all about deciding on a simple objective, but executing it was far from easy. I had to say goodbye to everything that had defined me until that point. I had to find a new group of friends who would keep me on the straight and narrow – a tough choice to make when you're a teenager. And that needed every ounce of self-discipline I had. It meant developing a strong sense of personal leadership – I had chosen a new and unknown direction; sometimes that was lonely and demanded a lot of mental strength to stay on track. Maybe it was the fear of the alternative that kept me going. If it was that, I am grateful. It set me on a new course towards a destiny I could be proud of. This power of focus fuelled my success. I hadn't been a great student at school, because I didn't realise the benefits of passing exams, but now I could see a world of opportunity ahead of me, if I just knuckled down and stayed focused.

So there I was: a father at not even 20 years old, working full-time and studying accountancy at night school. Those circumstances catapulted me into adulthood when I made the choice to pursue a career and take my responsibilities seriously. I began to excel at both my work and my studies. My colleagues liked me because I got things done, didn't shy away from my obligations and followed through on my commitments. It wasn't easy, but I soon discovered that I actually *liked* to learn and also had a capacity for hard work. It took me six years to earn my accounting degree, and when I qualified I was given a company car and a raise. I began to taste success for the first time – and it made me hungry for more.

What was clear was that my future probably lay outside my home town. Yorkshire was still a textile and mining stronghold but the textile mills were closing down as the industry moved to Taiwan and Sri Lanka. Mines were also shutting down. It was a pretty bleak and volatile environment with massive inflation and factories scaling back to three-day weeks. I'll never forget the sight of a decorated ex-soldier who broke down when he was laid off. He could fight an enemy that he could see but he couldn't fight a future that had blindsided him.

It was also the dawn of something new. It was the early eighties and we were being fed a line that the sky was the limit, *greed was good* and anyone could 'make it' if they wanted it badly enough and worked hard enough. And I wanted it bad enough – so I started thinking about the possibility of working overseas.

I scanned the recruitment pages in the accounting journals, which is how I joined a fantastic Lebanese company called Abela. They had an office in Savile Row in London – and it was there that I smelled the excitement of 'international'. And knew it was where I wanted to be. They ran hotel and catering businesses all over the world and also had contracts with major airports and large construction projects. More importantly, they liked me! I began my international journey as the financial controller of a hotel in the Sudan, which was followed by assignments in Bahrain, Kuwait, Jamaica and the Canary Islands, all of which were incredibly exotic locations for a young lad from Yorkshire. I loved the travel, and I soon found that I had a way with people from all cultures. Maybe it was my essential simplicity. Maybe it was my ability to get the job done in a way that helped other people achieve their goals, or maybe it was just that I find people and their challenges extremely interesting.

I realised that I was a pretty good General Manager – and so did my boss! In the Sudan and then in Jamaica, when the manager there went on holiday for a month, he put me in charge. I loved it. In my career I've been lucky enough to have many jobs I've loved, which I think has been a big part of my success – it means that even my worst days are bearable, because I know that I'm one of the lucky few people who completely loves what they do. At the end of the day, it's simple – you can't be great at something if you don't like doing it.

Amazingly, and somewhat accidentally, at the age of 27, I discovered my forte. I learned that I had a talent for turning things round: I was a natural troubleshooter. Others ran away from problems, but I ran towards them, because I grasped the essential elements of success:

- Rigorously dig into the detail.
- Get close to the people who are aware of what's going on.
- Make sure that the basics are completed and recorded.
- Identify the right process and execute it.
- Don't be afraid to call out people who are not doing their jobs properly.
- Deliver what you promise you will.
- Get it right for your customers – whatever it takes.

I had learned that if you do the fundamentals right you can be confident that the problem will be resolved. If you present things honestly and accurately, you'll find a way to make things right. If things are in a mess, on the other hand, you won't be able to draw a plan. In business, the financial roadmap must be clear. The challenge is to have the patience and tenacity to stay the course.

I was sent to work wherever a business was in crisis. I loved the work, but unfortunately it ended my marriage – we separated shortly after I started working abroad. This experience taught me the important lesson that shared values are crucial in both the home and the workplace. Unless both parties have shared priorities, a relationship will generally not last.

Then, in 1985, at the age of 30, I found the perfect company for me: DHL Express, the company that would become something like my soul-mate. I set about becoming an expert in the international express business – an expert is an ordinary person who consistently seeks out knowledge in a specialised field and applies it.

At the beginning of 1987, something else happened that would change my life forever. I met the woman who would become my wife. Her name is Gigi. I was meeting with the DHL financial team in Cairo, Egypt. About halfway through the meeting, a woman entered. She apologised for disturbing the meeting, whispered a few words to one of the people present and left. I felt like I had been struck by a thunderbolt. She was quite simply the most beautiful woman that I had ever seen.

I discovered that Gigi was a salesperson for DHL in Alexandria. So I arranged to visit the city under the guise of collecting outstanding debts from late-paying customers. Gigi and I drove around pursuing payments and learning about each other. The more I learned about her, the more I fell for her.

Luckily for me, the feeling was mutual. We got married in 1989. We have three children together – Danielle, Nicole and Alexander. Whatever else DHL has given me, Gigi is my greatest gift.

As Gigi tells the story:

I was in Cairo for my cousin's wedding. I popped in to see the finance guy. A few days later, I heard that Ken wanted to come to Alexandria to collect outstanding money from customers. I said that we had no problem collecting money. But I was told that he was coming shortly. I had to quickly call companies and tell them that they hadn't paid for two weeks so we were coming to see them. It was only two years ago that Ken admitted that the real reason he came was to see me.

I could see how much Ken loved me. It was in his eyes. I could see that he had such a kind heart. That's what hit me. He was in love with Egypt and he was obviously in love with me. There was not a drop of annoyance in him. That's what I fell in love with – his kindness. I never thought that he would become CEO because he's not an overly ambitious person. He's just so nice.

If you have some talent and can give great results to those who employ you, you can create a reputation for delivery and dependability. And when you have this kind of reputation and are happy in yourself, you are able to give and achieve more. It's a virtuous circle – if you can tap into your own drive and motivation and combine that with a natural approach, the result is that your employers will love you and reward you well for your efforts.

Twenty-four years later, in 2009, I became global CEO of the organisation. I didn't set out to achieve this role, but my career at DHL has enabled me to realise my natural talent and to unlock the company's huge potential, rather like the manager of a professional sports team who discovers the right team formation and is able to lead it to multiple championship wins. Unlike motivational speakers, I resist saying something new for the sake of it: instead I am quite happy to say the right thing over and over again – and I am prepared to do so for as long as it takes for people to respond.

MY PHILOSOPHY

What do you need to know about me as you read about my career in this book? Here are a few things that I regularly get called:

A TURNAROUND SPECIALIST. It's just who I am and what I do, but I can't deny that it felt good when I was recognised as the number one Turnaround Manager in Germany by the prestigious *Wirtschaftswoche* magazine. This sort of recognition is always nice – but the numbers tell the real story; the consultants A.T. Kearney say with confidence that we have delivered one of the biggest turnarounds in the history of transportation: that's the sort of pat on the back that I'm happy to take.

A CUSTOMER CHAMPION. If you cut me open, you would find the word 'customer' running right through me like a stick of rock. But I'm not just *interested* in our customers – they are such a priority for me that I'm proud to have created an 'Insanely Customer-centric Culture' where my team of 100,000 feel literally sick if we let even one customer down. It's my passion and it pays dividends – our market share has increased from 29 per cent in 2008 to 38 per cent in 2018.

A PEOPLE LEADER. It takes a team to transform a company, and all great teams need inspiration, tactics, passion and the skills to play at their best. That's why I pioneered something called CIS (Certified International Specialist) – the world's most global culture engagement programme, which has been rolled out to 100,000 employees in 220 countries and 47 languages (I'll talk about this in more detail later, see Chapter 10). It cost the company an arm and a leg, but was it worth it? Without doubt! DHL Express has world-leading Employee Opinion Survey scores, and we've improved participation in active leadership from 60 per cent in 2008 to 87 per cent in 2018 and Employee Engagement from 63 per cent to 88 per cent over the same period. Our crowning glory came in 2018 when we were recognised by *Fortune* and Great Place to Work as the sixth best place to work in the world.

A SHAREHOLDER ADVOCATE. The analysts and shareholders have started calling me 'the Singing CEO', following my rendition of 'Billionaire' at my first Capital Markets Day. And year after year I've been able to give them something to sing about, improving DHL Express's EBIT (earnings before interest and taxes) from a loss of €2.2 billion in 2008 to a profit of €1.95 billion in 2018. Express is now the highest margin business in the express market (12 per cent).

A GLOBAL CITIZEN. I'm proud that I run the most international company in the world; I also happen to think we're the best in the world. It's critical that we are representative of the world at its best, which is why we take so seriously our responsibility to actively and positively build a better, fairer and sustainable world.

SOCIALLY RESPONSIBLE. My team is amazing – they are full of pride, passion and love – and that needs recognition and celebration. That's why I set up DHL's Got Heart, a friendly internal competition, to encourage employees to support the charitable activities that they most care about. And my amazing colleagues always come into their own when the world experiences natural or man-made disasters – we're ideally placed, because we know a lot about airports, we know a lot about logistics and we know how to keep our heads in a crisis. That's why our Disaster Response Team (DRT), which is made up of hundreds of highly trained volunteers, is able to take over airports and provide logistics support to countries in times of the most severe and devastating crisis.

RADICALLY SIMPLE

Steve Jobs often talked about simplicity as being the ultimate sophistication. He said:

> *Simple can be harder than complex: you have to work hard to get your thinking clean to make it simple. But it's worth it in the end because once you get there, you can move mountains.*

Jobs was light years better than I could ever dream of being in his thinking – but the lessons in this one quote are big enough to transform a business. When I took over as CEO in 2009, this simple message was ringing in my ears as I started to get my head around the phenomenal task of transforming the world's most international company. That's when I created SELF Reflection, an approach that guides a great deal of my thinking and decision-making. It was instrumental in my turnaround of DHL, but also works equally well for the operation and tactical decisions that we make every day as business leaders. It's at the heart of how I have had such success in improving the fortunes of businesses.

S IS FOR SIMPLICITY, which is the overriding principle behind my app-roach to work – it's the framework that provides the architecture of what you want to build. Knowing what you *should* do in a difficult situation is easy, but actually doing it requires you to make tough decisions and live with the consequences. When I was faced with the imposing task of turning DHL around, I knew we had to get back to our roots – we had invented a business but we'd been distracted from it, so we needed to get back to the simple idea that we were famous for.

E IS FOR EXECUTION, which is just as important as the strategy itself. It is the discipline needed to get the right things done, which requires a comprehensive understanding of a business, its people and its processes. When you believe you have made the right decision and are following the best path for you, execution is much easier; you can see clearly what's important to do and what you should stop doing. If I've learned one thing in my career, it's the importance of meticulous and determined execution. At DHL I needed a clear turnaround strategy that everyone would be able to execute. I needed to make sure that the whole company was focused on 'doing things' – the right things; that wins out every time for me.

L IS FOR LEADERSHIP, which then empowers and supports every level of the organisation to perform and improve. All leaders should be experts and motivators, and leadership starts at home: if you don't have the personal discipline to lead yourself to where you need to go, how will you be able to lead others? Taking charge of yourself, managing yourself, motivating yourself and organising yourself to succeed is the start of your journey to becoming a great leader. I couldn't do this on my own at DHL – I needed to surround myself with the right leaders, who were experts *and* motivators, in order for us to be the Chief *Energy* Officers of the organisation and deliver amazing results.

F IS FOR FOCUS, which keeps the organisation on track – as a result a company can grow, both in terms of revenue and profitability. The task may seem daunting, so keeping a single-minded focus on achieving short-term outcomes keeps you on the right path and helps you to ignore the enormity of the task ahead. My colleagues at DHL had to be in no doubt about where we were going and how we would get there – I needed a simple turnaround strategy that brought people, service and profit together – written in simple terms, shared widely with everyone in the company and delivered by all.

REFLECTION is the next step in the process, and ensures that you stay relevant; you review, learn and adapt. Is it really as simple as that? I think it is. But what are some of the biggest takeaways for me?

- To design and implement a great strategy, especially the kind of turnaround strategies I'm now known for, you need an intimate knowledge of your business, its operating units and, most importantly, its customers and its culture.

- You also need the capacity and discipline to step outside that, to remove yourself from what you think you know to be true and genuinely reflect on the good, the bad and the ugly elements of your business.

- You need to be able to reflect and then use those reflections to create a vision of what you want your business to become, and it has to be a vision you believe in with all your heart and that will propel you forwards, even during the toughest of times.

- Then you have to tap in to and trust your gut feeling for the right things to do that will make your dream a reality. That feeling will serve you best if you have a deep and practical knowledge of your business and a passion for getting things right for your customers and people. Great CEOs do this – and they also write and communicate simple, relevant, inspiring strategies that can mobilise hundreds of thousands of people.

- The ultimate question is 'Do I really understand what the customer requirements are and do we honestly have the capability to deliver an economically viable solution?'

But back to the title of this book, *Radical Simplicity*. The concept of simplicity has existed in management literature for some time, but I think that, in our increasingly complex world, it has been forgotten or lost its pre-eminence. During my career, like all aspiring managers, I was a voracious reader of management books, and what struck me most about them was the simplicity and consistency of the messages that they all seemed to espouse. I'm older and somewhat wiser now and, as a result, keep only the three books on my shelf that have helped me the most in my career – they are the following (along with their main messages):

Mean Business: How I Save Bad Companies and Make Good Companies Great by Albert J. Dunlap (1996)

- Business is remarkably simple. Get the right management team, cut costs, focus on the core business and get a real strategy (and not one designed by consultants).
- Cost is always your enemy. You have to get to a good cost position and get there quickly – you should never cut an hourly worker before you have dealt with the staff in your corporate headquarters.
- Focus on a handful of goals. If you set too many, you will fail. Focus like a laser, sell everything and focus on your core business.

Execution: The Discipline of Getting Things Done by Larry Bossidy and Ram Charan (2002)

- Set clear goals and priorities. Effective leaders focus on a very few clear priorities that everyone can grasp. Focusing on three or four priorities will produce the best results from the resources you have to hand.
- Strive for simplicity in general. One thing you'll notice about leaders who execute is that they speak simply and directly.
- Can the business execute the strategy? An astonishing number of strategies fail because leaders don't make a realistic assessment of whether the organisation can execute the plan.

How the Mighty Fall: And Why Some Companies Never Give In by Jim Collins (2009)

- A great company is more likely to die of indigestion from too much opportunity than starvation from too little. If you want to reverse decline, you should be rigorous about what *not* to do.
- Dramatic leaps in performance come when an executive team of exceptional leaders coalesce and make a series of outstanding, supremely well-executed decisions. According to Jim Collins's research, over 90 per cent of CEOs who led companies 'from good to great' came from inside organisations.

These are the core pieces of advice that I have lived by and which drove our turnaround, but they are just as relevant to the businesses and business leaders of today as they were 10 to 15 years ago. And in one way or another, they all begin with simplicity – and end in Radical Simplicity.

KEY LEARNING

- Rigorously dig into the detail.
- Make sure the basics are recorded and completed.
- Identify the right process and execute it.
- Don't be afraid to call out people who aren't doing their job properly.
- Get it right for your customers whatever it takes.
- Work hard to get your thinking clear to make it simple.
- Focus on a few clear priorities that everyone can grasp.
- Create a not-to-do list, rather than a to-do list.

CHAPTER 3:
A SIMPLE HISTORY
OF DHL
FOUNDED ON DISRUPTION

Death, taxes and DHL – the only certainties in life
Early Advertising Campaign

It is hard to imagine, but before 1969 there was no international express industry. Thanks to the entrepreneurial spirit of DHL's three founders, a new industry was born in San Francisco in that year, and it would change how world trade worked forever. The company has had a colourful history – it grew rapidly, had to fight global postal monopolies, almost went bankrupt more times than it would like to admit, became a massive brand name and was eventually acquired by the German Post Office. But today, as a mature disruptor, it's still sticking to the pioneering ideals and principles of its founders and is playing a pivotal role in the rapid growth of e-commerce around the world.

Just months after the first moon landing, DHL began operating the world's first international door-to-door express delivery service. When Adrian Dalsey, Larry Hillblom and Robert Lynn established the company they also invented an industry. They had no capital, but they did have a simple 'disruptive' idea: to deliver shipping documents by air so that they arrived at customs offices before the freight, enabling goods to pass through customs with fewer delays. They were classic entrepreneurs, and started moving shipping documents to Hawaii, so ships could pre-clear and save demurrage charges. It was a truly simple and inspired business model. With a suitcase and credit card, they travelled wherever their customers wanted them to go. It worked so well that their business expanded with an unprecedented growth curve – opening offices in places such as the Philippines, Hong Kong, Japan, the UK, Iran and Mexico.

DHL began with no capital, but the company always had big dreams and big ideas. It was precocious from the start, and challenged the established postal services in its quest to move documents faster across the world. And if it could be done with documents, surely they could invent international express for parcels?

In 1977, the parcel product was introduced, which kick-started another massive growth spurt. Rapid international expansion continued, with offices opening in Germany, Korea, Nigeria, South Africa, Argentina, Turkey and in Eastern Europe. At that time, DHL had operations in 24 countries in total. Its customers included such big companies as Seatrain Lines, Phillips Petroleum, IBM, Kodak, Standard Oil, Bank of America, American Express, United California Bank, Chase Manhattan and First National City Bank (now known as Citibank).

By 1985, the company was still young but it was hard-working and saw no limits to its rapid growth. While it wasn't yet making money, the focus was simple – to rapidly build a globally recognised brand that was famous for providing great service. Between 1989 and 1999, the company grew by more that 1,500 per cent, doubling its customer base to more than half a million – and was operating in 142 countries and territories.

In 1990, UPS made an approach to buy DHL, but the company turned it down. When 'professional' management was brought in from the outside to increase efficiency, it resulted in fiefdoms around the world and no network culture at a senior management level, but the front line and middle management were entrepreneurial and dedicated, and continued to grow the company opening another 32 offices.

In 1992, DHL formed a joint venture with Lufthansa, Japan Airlines and Nissho Iwai, a major import-export company. All sides tried hard to make the partnership work, but the hoped-for synergies proved elusive and the engagement was called off. By this time the company was operating in 193 countries and territories.

In 1995 Larry Hillblom, one of the co-founders of DHL and the driving force behind the company's growth, died tragically in a plane crash in the Western Pacific – although his body was never found. He was only 52 years old, but his simple idea had completely revolutionised the way the world did business. The company continued to grow, opening offices in Mauritius and Moldova to bring the total number of countries to 218. We often wondered if there was anywhere else we could be, and there was!

In 1999, 30 years after the company had been established, we found ourselves in 227 countries and territories. From then on, we could legitimately call ourselves the 'most international company in the world', a title we are rightly proud of and have retained to this day – it's said that we're available in more countries than Coca-Cola, American Express and the United Nations!

In 2002, DHL was taken over by Deutsche Post. At that point it was losing €150 million a year, having never learned how to effectively manage the financial complexity of a global network and operate as a harmonious whole rather than an affiliation of regions. The US was a substantial loss-maker and strategically weak. The original founders were no longer alive, and the lack of capital and investment that were required to expand made it the perfect time for existing shareholders to withdraw their investment. It seemed ironic that DHL had fought ferociously with postal authorities for years before deciding to merge with one, but the company's irresponsible fiscal behaviour left it with no choice. Still, to celebrate, its colours changed from red and white to the iconic red and yellow that is still prominent today. However, unsurprisingly, the union proved difficult; integrating it with multiple domestic acquisitions in the United States, Canada, the UK, France, Spain and China was an incredibly complex undertaking.

By 2008, with the global financial crisis on the horizon, DHL Express made a record loss of €2.2 billion. DHL was haemorrhaging cash in the

US – losing over €100 million every single month. Of the 15 people on the US board, not one had domestic US express experience. The losses were causing increasing consternation in the Group headquarters in Germany – it was feared that they might bring down the whole of Deutsche Post if the situation continued much longer. A succession of people was brought in to turn the situation around but none of them were able to do so, being committed to improving the status quo rather than making any more substantive changes.

In 2009, DHL was 40 years old, yet had never been consistently profitable. The bottom line was measured in terms of packages delivered and customers satisfied, rather than on return on assets. DHL focused on customer satisfaction, but never had the financial discipline to convert this satisfaction into profit. However, the company was one of the original start-ups in global business, and had never stopped feeling like one; its can-do culture and pioneering mentality of redefining what could be done was in its DNA, and its culture had always been about motivating people and giving them a chance to succeed if they worked hard, no matter where they came from.

In that year, I became global CEO determined to bring the organisation together 'As One'.

I introduced the concept of SELF Reflection:

Simplicity	International express only.
Execution	'We have a strategic plan. It's called doing things.'
Leadership	Halved the corporate board to six people, everyone an express expert and multifunctional.
Focus	A detailed plan to 2015 was laid out in a brochure, including financials. Later extended to 2020.

Reflection

DHL Express had weathered a huge crisis but needed to grow up as a business. We decided to focus on becoming the best in the world in the area of business that was going to grow most rapidly – the thing that we knew we were best at and had pioneered 40 years before – time-definite international shipping. We focused on the international business and uniting the network, aiming to make it the Greatest International Express Company on the Planet.

The plan was simple. It was called Focus – focused on our unique strength, that we're the most international company in the world, and we should put all our effort into maintaining our international lead. It had four Focus pillars: Motivated People who deliver Great Service Quality, resulting in Loyal Customers, who are the only sure driver of a Profitable Network. We put our goals in writing and held ourselves accountable for the results.

In 2011, the turnaround was producing such good results that we introduced the 'Speed of Yellow' global advertising campaign which launched in 42 key markets worldwide. This reimagining of DHL's famous original ads featured the iconic 'Ain't No Mountain High Enough' soundtrack and demonstrated our expertise in the fashion, automotive and technology industries.

By 2012, we were firing on all cylinders, mastering the discipline, processes and customer focus to become a global winner and making €1 billion in earnings before interest and tax – and we have continued to grow ever since.

In 2013 we had our first global 'Kick-on' conference for 1,200 leaders in Dubai to celebrate our success and declared our commitment to taking the business to a whole new level.

In 2017, we generated €1.62 billion EBIT, a billion of cash flow as well as investing €1 billion in capex (capital expenditure). We were now billionaires by several different measures, and all it had taken was a bit of Focus! We've got all our plans in place to 2020 and I have no doubt that we will hit those ambitious goals as well.

In 2018, the business performed even better, delivering a record EBIT margin of 12 per cent and €1.95 billion EBIT.

In 2019, DHL Express celebrated its fiftieth year in logistics. The 'mature disruptor' had turned into the elder statesman, financially strong and in a good position to help the products of the e-commerce global boom be delivered on time consistently. I handed over to my successor as global CEO, John Pearson, knowing the business I love was in safe hands.

Today, DHL Express employs 100,000 people around the world, in over 220 countries. We are the world's leading international express logistics company: in 2018, we shipped 150 million packages for 2.8 million active customers to 120,000 destinations and fielded 66 million inbound calls with 62,000 vehicles and 250 dedicated aircraft. We have three global hubs, in Leipzig, Hong Kong and Cincinnati, and 15 regional hubs around the world. We have an IT network that connects the DHL global network at all times, and we track packages through 12 million checkpoints every day. We have two global data centres in Prague and Kuala Lumpur, and over 200 global applications. It's an interlinked business of mind-boggling complexity, but at its heart, it's also very simple: we deliver packages all over the world for our customers, meeting their specific deadlines. DHL, a company that had once been an ugly duckling, has become a beautiful swan and the jewel in the Deutsche Post crown.

THE EVOLUTION OF OUR AVIATION NETWORK

No review of how DHL became the business it is today would be complete without a look at how we created the concept of the virtual airline, which is based on local arrangements and global partnerships in over 220 countries and territories around the world. The journey to developing this awesome network required innovation, expert planning and vision. In the first few decades of DHL, our fleet incorporated a variety of aircraft, each performing a different role that was required for a growing network. This included everything from moving small consignments quickly between neighbouring countries use the Beechcraft, to moving larger loads across the Atlantic in DC-8s. Many of these aircraft were branded up and DHL's iconic three letters started to become a regular feature on the flight paths of the world.

The way DHL built its aviation network was one of the most unique aspects of the business. At a time when most airlines were operated by national authorities, DHL challenged the status quo. As a company that was emerging around the world without an established structure or even a recognisable home base, we created our aviation network with typical DHL common sense. Here is the story of how our aviation network has evolved since the early days of the company.

The 1970s

Throughout the 1970s, DHL's international express operations were using on-board couriers who carried documents as luggage, working with both late cut-offs at origin and achieving fast customs clearance at the destination.

The 1980s

As volumes increased, DHL adapted the courier baggage model to secure more capacity. Standard airfreight was also used where the longer cut-off and recovery wouldn't impact overall transit time.

However, over time, congestion in the baggage halls became an issue. The introduction of express clearance facilities at major airports, starting with London Heathrow, addressed this issue. These, however, were for baggage only – airfreight still had to go through the slower recovery routines. So we began to look for a way to process freight at the same speed as baggage, which eventually led to DHL being granted airside access, removing the need for on-board couriers. This lowered our network line haul costs and by the late 1980s, we had airside access at all primary transfer points.

In some key sectors, the flying courier model reached its limit much earlier. Bahrain to Dhahran in Saudi Arabia was a key line, but had just one flight each morning to connect to the long-haul traffic from Europe and Asia. So DHL put its own aircraft on this route. In 1979 we introduced the first owned and operated network flight in the US, following a reduction in night-time flights by the big domestic carriers. To compete domestically, we set up a 'hub-and-spoke' system with dedicated aircraft that operated to our timings. Initially, a range of third-party providers was used, but they were phased out as DHL Airways grew its own fleet.

Our next major expansion was in Europe, where there was a lack of commercial airline night flights. The same hub-and-spoke system was introduced here, with Brussels at the centre due to its road reach and absence of aircraft night-noise constraints. A small Belgian commuter carrier, EAT, was acquired in 1985 as the focal point for DHL in Europe, developing and managing the portfolio of traffic rights for our fast-growing European network. Compared to the US, the shorter distances across Europe allowed for turbo-prop planes, so we bought and converted a fleet of ten Convairs. We began adding 20-tonne Boeing 727s on the bigger European routes in the 1990s, which combined with the use of road and wholesale freight air cargo sales, smoothed the increase in capacity and enabled us to reduce our European line haul costs.

The 1990s

By the late 1980s, flying couriers were being phased out. The Cincinnati and Brussels hubs were now operational and a dedicated flight connecting the two was needed. DHL's first intercontinental link was a shared flight with EMS (the European postal competitor) between New York and Brussels. As volumes grew, we started to use DC-8 aircraft, initially with third-party partners ATI, then Kalitta, and finally with DHL Airways in the mid 1990s. With the US and Europe expanding, an intra-Asia network was initiated in Manila in 1995. Using Air Micronesia's fifth-freedom traffic rights, Continental operated Boeing 727s for DHL. The whole operation was then shifted to Hong Kong in 2000, with Cathay Pacific providing space on Airbus A330s, and by 2003 the Cathay Pacific joint venture with Air Hong Kong was operating new A300-600s.

During the 1990s, volumes grew between 30 and 440 per cent. Our intercontinental network continued to rely on commercial airline services with DHL taking blocked space on carriers with suitable schedules. However, the prospect of a lack of cargo airline space on a number of lanes, especially out of Asia, started to become a concern in the late 1990s

In May 1997, DHL Aviation was also started in sub-Saharan Africa, with a small team of four people based in Zimbabwe. At the time the aircraft fleet consisted of only two Cessna C402s serving a small number of routes. In time, the fleet would expand to include DC-8s, Boeing 727s and Boeing 767s, linking 34 countries, with over 1,400 flights a month.

Back in Europe, aircraft noise pollution at night led to some European airports introducing night curfews. Given the noise generated by the older Boeing 727s, we began replacing them with newer Boeing 757s, and by the end of the mid 2000s we had 34 in service across Europe.

The 2000s

In 2005, our GAS (Global Aviation Strategy) was developed to address the international expansion of competitors, matching their flying rights and service capability. On the Trans-Pacific route, DHL acquired a 49 per cent equity stake in Polar Air, which held a number of Trans-Pacific and intra-Asia-Pacific fifth-freedom rights, facilitating our air operations, both within Asia-Pacific and the US. A Polar Air joint venture with Atlas Air was established with Boeing 747s, strengthening DHL's connection between Asia and the United States.

Preparations for a partnership with German carrier Lufthansa Cargo began in March 2004 under the name of AeroLogic. Between 2004 and 2009, the joint venture used a block space arrangement which gave DHL 47 per cent of the space aboard seven MD-11s. In 2009, six Boeing 767s were purchased, becoming the backbone of DHK, the DHL-owned airline based at the UK's East Midlands Hub.

When DHL withdrew from the US domestic market in 2008, our airline operations were drastically scaled back from 120 to 20 aircraft. Our original agreements with ASTAR (former DHL Airways) and ABX were ended and ASTAR terminated operations. Despite this, ABX Air, along with Atlas and Kalitta, remain our three main operators in the US today, with 24 Boeing 767s between them.

The 2010s

In 2012, we entered a multi-year contract with Southern Air to provide complementary services to our AeroLogic fleet with four Boeing 777 freight planes. The fuel efficiency, range and capacity of these aircraft connected our services via the key hubs in Cincinnati, Leipzig and Hong Kong. The decade also saw the purchase of 20 Airbus A300-600s in Europe and six in Asia-Pacific, which improved our fleet capabilities, service quality and profitability. More recently, in 2018 DHL strengthened its unmatched international network by purchasing 14 new Boeing 777 frieght planes, investments that allow us to meet increasing global express demand and serve more markets with non-stop flights.

I've outlined the story of DHL's relationship with aviation not to try and impress you with the magnitude of our operation, but to provide an insight into the way we think as a company. As I mentioned earlier, there has never been a time when vast amounts of capital have been available to the network, which has meant that our investment decisions have generally always been geared towards the most practical solution. When on-board couriers were no longer able to handle the volume of documents that we needed to transport in the 1970s, we consolidated the individual items and sent them as airfreight, on the proviso that this wouldn't impact their on-time delivery for the customer – those that would be affected continued to be transported as hand luggage.

When turbo-props were a viable alternative to more expensive jet-engine aircraft, we opted for this cost-effective solution as long as the customers' interests were safeguarded. It wasn't about 'future-proofing' our operation – it was about employing the most pragmatic solution that met everyone's needs. We formed partnerships with other carriers, shared flights and purchased space from third parties as a means of delivering the best service possible. The customers' satisfaction was our primary objective, which remains true to this day.

We now own and operate more than 250 aircraft, which fly in and out of over 500 airports in every corner of the globe. We're constantly upgrading them to meet environmental and fuel-efficiency regulations, which will enable us to reduce our reliance on fossil fuels and take us further towards our target of becoming the first logistics provider in the world with net-zero carbon emissions by 2050. This is a practical move that is aligned to the demands on our customers, and proof that you can operate a greener business without sacrificing cost savings and service quality.

CHAPTER 4:
CALL THE TROUBLESHOOTER
THE MIDDLE EAST, ASIA AND CANADA 1985-2006

The three rules of work:
Out of clutter find Simplicity
From discord find Harmony
In the middle of difficulty lies opportunity
Albert Einstein

My career with DHL began in Bahrain in 1985. I spent most of my first year working in Saudi Arabia and then went to Egypt, before returning to Bahrain as the Regional Finance Manager and then going to Yemen when the Country Manager there went on leave. I also helped to set up DHL in Libya. It was an exciting time – DHL was at the time a pioneer in some of the most volatile countries in the world, and it was thrilling to be a part of it. I felt like an adventurer whose job was to establish a financial frontier. I learned that the only way I could encourage freewheeling professionals to listen to me was to know their jobs as well as they did. In fact, I had to know their jobs even better than they did, because I was responsible for laying down processes for them to follow.

When I first joined DHL in the Middle East, the financial records held by the office were incomplete. The way in which the office there was run was certainly entrepreneurial, but it also felt undisciplined – it was almost like no one had a true perspective of what was actually going on. In fact, almost 20 years later, when the company was acquired by Deutsche Post, that would still be DHL's biggest problem. It had always had great people who were highly talented, but financial rigour was almost totally lacking. That was a match made in heaven for me: I was exactly what the doctor ordered.

A big part of my job was to introduce order to disorder. I needed to think like an entrepreneur and an accountant at the same time. I knew I could bring the financial discipline to match the company's operational capability, which made me stand out from my counterparts. The company welcomed people who could think for themselves and offer different perspectives, and I became their troubleshooting Chief Financial Officer – someone who would think like a businessman first and a financial expert second. In a company that was expanding so quickly you needed to think and act fast – and I was good at that.

In the late 1980s, UPS was exploring the possibility of buying DHL. They started looking at the Middle East and discussing profit models with us. We used to work according to a model called Notional Results (which meant local revenue minus local costs), but DHL as a whole didn't understand the global profitability of door-to-door delivery. As a Regional Finance Manager, I was on the global finance board, and it soon became clear to me that most of the regional offices and the global head office lacked the level of sophis-tication that a complex company like DHL needed. That seemed to me to be one of the main reasons that the company was not making money: you cannot manage what you cannot monitor. Operational excellence must be matched by financial sophistication. I found the whole challenge incredibly appealing: everywhere I looked, there were opportunities to improve how the company functioned.

Just before the start of the Gulf War in 1991, I was promoted to Regional Manager of the Middle East. My boss at the time believed in delegating as much as possible, and in giving the staff who worked for him as much respon-sibility as they had proved they could handle. I was keen for as much as he chose to give me. It wasn't work to me; it was an opportunity to see how far I could go. And the further I went, the further I wanted to go.

One of the first things I focused on was the quality of service we were offering; we began a number of quality assurance programmes to ensure that we picked up and delivered on time. It was around this time that I first met and became inspired by Charlie Dobbie, the current Executive Vice President of Global Network Operations for IT and Aviation at DHL. He was working in Australia at the time, but had seen that the best data on operational quality and financial performance in the company was coming out of the Middle East. He wanted to learn how our processes worked and then apply them everywhere. It was ironic that one of the most chaotic regions was providing such reliable data, especially in the aftermath of the Gulf War, but it also proved that the right processes can transcend any environment if the discipline is there. Charlie is an inspiration when it comes to service quality; he experiences a visceral reaction when things go wrong and talks about feeling sick in the pit of his stomach if he lets a customer or employee down. I think of him as the archetypal DHL employee – he lights up any room he walks into with his passion, dedication and care for the company, his energy is infectious and he is a force for good across the whole organisation. He loves our business, our customers and our employees – and he inspires everyone around him to feel the same way.

A great example of DHL's commitment to results actually occurred *because* of the Gulf War. When the war was over, DHL was the first company to return to Kuwait, where a staff member in the DHL finance department found the equipment that had been disturbed by the Iraqi army and managed to invoice clients for all the shipments that had been made just before the invasion. That's the kind of dedication to providing first-rate service that warms my heart! As a company, DHL has always practised FILO (First In, Last Out) during times of crisis.

It was during my time in the Middle East that I had the pleasure of meeting David Wilson who joined us in Saudi Arabia in 1996 and progressed through many positions until eventually beoming Executive Vice President Global Sales. Unfortunately, in 2016 he was diagnosed with glioblastoma, a severe brain tumour. This is an aggressive type of cancer with survival rates beyond a year set at just 25 per cent. He left us to live in Canada with his wife and five children where he continues to defy all the odds. Dave was also caught up in the terrorist attack in Dharan in 2004 when armed insurgents killed numerous people on his compound, but his quick thinking and action saved him and his family, which is why he named his daughter 'Hope'.

In Dave's words:

I started with DHL in Saudi Arabia in 1996. I was a front-line salesperson. Ken was the Middle East Area Director. I met him during a Bahrain relay marathon that DHL participated in. The thing that struck me was how easily Ken mixed with everyone – especially after the race when he showed up at the pub and had a few drinks with all the lads.

Although I had a good relationship with Ken while I was at DHL, he communicates with me now more than ever before. In fact, after my family, Ken communicates with me more than anyone else. That says a lot about Ken's commitment to people and relationships for life.

Whenever Ken visited the businesses, he never went through the front door. He would always go in through the back door. He would walk through operations and customer service. Then he would visit the leadership office. The one thing that Ken and I always agreed on: we're a courier company. Anything that didn't further that function should be stripped away.

Ken was remarkable at remembering names, people and places. He is also very loyal to people who serve the company well. He forgives them for many shortfalls if they commit to the Four Pillars and stand the test of time. However, if people are in senior positions and they show that they are not in touch with the front line, Ken can be brutal. I have seen him get really angry with leaders who betray their lack of knowledge or understanding of the business. The most important thing to him is always the care and support for the front line.

I was Regional Manager in the Middle East until 1997, when the world was hit by the dot-com crisis. the company rationalised its operations around the world and I was transferred to Singapore to run finance for the Far East and Southeast Asia, the Middle East and Africa.

I stayed in Asia from 1998 until 2004. In this turbulent decade I came into my own. I found myself as CFO in Asia Pacific and the Middle East during the currency and export crisis in the region. It was an exciting part of the world and a great training ground for a would-be future global CEO, requiring focus and discipline to meet demanding financial targets while investing heavily in new facilities and infrastructure to build a market-leading platform. It's also where I learned a critical lesson regarding the power of pricing. A number of currencies, such as the Thai baht and the Korean won, had depreciated by more than 50 per cent, so we had to increase prices substantially in the recessionary market, which meant price hikes of between 50 and 70 per cent. It was also the beginning of what are now annual pricing reviews, which look at issues such as inflation, currency devaluation and costs, including wage increases, to refine our price position globally.

In my last two years in the role, I was the Asian lead on STAR, a group-wide value enhancement programme that created a uniform brand presence around the world and, through process and scale economies, created a low-cost structure for Deutsche Post DHL. It was a baptism of fire for me in global brand-building and cost restructuring, but I loved every minute of it. It also meant that I had to work alongside some of the people at Deutsche Post who had been most influential in the acquisition of DHL in 2002, another happy accident that helped me on my journey to becoming global CEO.

After my time in Asia Pacific and the Middle East, I was asked, in 2005, to move to Canada. DHL had just merged with a successful express logistics company there called Loomis, but the combined operation was losing money. It represented a sideways move for me because Canada was a relatively small part of the company, but they needed me to do the job, and I saw it as an opportunity to have another adventure. I had never worked in Canada before, and I was curious to see if, as the company's General Manager in that country, I could succeed in turning another situation around.

One of the most valuable lessons that my experience in Canada taught me was that the best career moves are not always upwards – sometimes an assignment adds perspective to your CV and enables you to develop valuable skills. Canada was where my obsession began with placing the customer at the heart of everything that we did. I made the decision not to take on any new customers until we got our house in order, after a customer threatened to leave us because we were not even able to invoice them accurately. That was a real wake-up call, and reminded me that there is nothing basic about the basics; service quality and customer loyalty are inseparable, and you can't expect the latter without providing the former.

Unlike other territories around the world where we were dominant, in Canada DHL was a distant third to UPS and FedEx. However, I didn't have time to worry about size or branding: my mission was to first get the business onto a firm footing. Once we had turned the business around, we quickly rebranded all the Loomis trucks in DHL colours. I personally travelled the routes and offered couriers a brand-new DHL shirt and $10 in cash if they immediately changed their uniform. I think this sort of action has become a signature of mine: I always try to engage our front-line staff in a way that not only gets results, but also generates a buzz in their community. If the CEO himself is willing to hit the streets and do whatever it takes to get couriers into DHL colours, then it shows everyone else that they should be willing to go to equal extremes. One thing is for sure: you can't build an outstanding business from behind a desk.

My time in Canada was a huge success and the company's fortunes there changed dramatically: within two years, we had converted a €45 million loss into a €12 million profit. The lesson I learned from the experience was that it is always preferable to fix things quickly, which means taking decisive action. This involved making some difficult decisions, including letting go of employees who didn't seem to care about customers sufficiently. One manager refused to handle customer complaints directly, feeling that it was beneath him, so I got involved in his place and took every call instead of him. The only way to lead is to lead by example. We also did everything we could to improve employee motivation and got our workforce excited about the business again. In most businesses, and especially in the delivery business, not enough investment is made in inspiring the front line, but I took the view that the front line is key to the bottom line. In our case, even a little bit of attention made a massive difference. We managed to convince the unions to align with our goals regarding quality of service, because they saw what a positive impact they could have on employees. Pride was a powerful stimulant in this regard – after all, no one wants to work for a company that they don't feel anything for. I saw people transforming before my eyes because they felt like they were an important part in a business that was changing for the better.

One of the key reasons I was able to make a difference was that people saw that I genuinely cared. Many managers say they care, when deep down in their hearts they don't – and their actions often belie their rhetoric. If you don't really feel it, you won't do it – it's as simple as that. This means that when taking on difficult assignments, you had better make sure that you care deeply about them. You need a passion for the grind so it sharpens you up rather than wears you down – the faint- or false-hearted never last.

The way to get the best out of your staff is not through 'command and control' tactics – it's by treating them as human beings whose well-being is just as important to you as your own, especially those who are on the front line. When things go wrong, it's important to remember that it is never their fault – it's always a management issue, and as a leader, you have to take responsibility for that on the chin, and you also have to be transparent in how you're trying to fix it. When I was working to improve the Canadian business, I was in constant communication with our stakeholders, both inside the company and out, and I also crisscrossed the 5,000 kilometre-wide country multiple times in a series of roadshows and consultations. All these efforts paid off. We earned the trust of everyone, even the sceptics, and this was reflected almost immediately in our financial results. I had learned an important lesson: not everyone can do great things every day, but everyone *can* do small things in a great way, every day.

After this change in approach, our front-line people stopped merely being pick up and delivery professionals and became much more our eyes and ears in the market. They told us when they saw a competitor's packages, they relayed what receptionists told them about how DHL compared to the competition and they also became vital at seeking out new opportunities for the business. That's when I made up my mind that, no matter what function people perform, everybody should behave as if they are in sales.

I love Canada, and I especially love the people there and their commitment to process and their desire to do what's fair. Canadians are champions of compromise and realise that a solution doesn't have to be perfect – it just has to be right for everyone. We were able to restore the Canadian business of DHL to profitability by building trust with our customers, our people and the unions. But although we had got our internal processes in order and became good, we were still far from great. We had managed to turn the business around, but there was still a feeling that we weren't yet as good as we could be.

While in Canada I had the opportunity to work with a world-class motivational speaker called Mike Lipkin. He really helped me develop my presentation skills and content, particularly for our front-line employees. He would become a regular companion on my journey to where I am today. People love him and his enthusiasm for life is contagious. He has his own stories of personal struggles but he has overcome them and built an amazing business and following.

The great thing about working with entrepreneurs in relatively small businesses is that you see their incredible customer-centricity and how much they focus on delivering exactly what the customer needs. I believe that working closely with them also instils a renewed sense of entrepreneurism in our more formal business environment.

My time in Canada also provided the perfect opportunity for me to see for myself just how bad things were for DHL across the border in the United States. I had a front-row seat, because it was one of the destinations that we shipped to most often. The US was draining the organisation's resources; the global board believed that the situation was under control, but I wasn't so sure. I would come back to slay that dragon a few years later, but my next assignment was already being formulated.

KEY LEARNING
- Service quality and customer loyalty are inseparable.
- You can't build outstanding businesses from behind a desk.
- Pride is a powerful motivating factor.
- Not everyone can do great things every day, but everyone *can* do small things in a great way.
- Make everyone a salesperson.

CHAPTER 5:
ALWAYS BE OPEN TO DESTINY

EEMEA 2005–2007

On the floor and in the field
Reducing cost, increasing yield
Lots of people interaction
And total customer satisfaction.
  Ken Allen

When I was asked by the CEO of DHL Express to take over the EEMEA region (Eastern Europe, the Middle East and Africa) in 2005, it felt in a way like I was coming home, because of the previous time I had spent working in the Middle East. It would also be one of the best times of my career.

Although the EEMEA business was in a healthy state, the previous leadership hadn't focused sufficiently strongly on people. The staff there may have been performing satisfactorily, but they weren't especially motivated. Over the next two years, I aimed to make 'motivated people' my top priority. I invested in training, introduced regional meetings, compensation and infrastructure, all with the ambition of building a powerful esprit de corps. I travelled around the region and met as many people as I could, sharing my passion for the company and the positive impact we could have on the world. I also explained my history with DHL and how it worked. By then I had been with the company for some 20 years, which meant that I knew the business as well as anyone, and I was passionate about the services that we offered. Of course I focused on the numbers, but I didn't ever hesitate to express my emotions.

The people who worked for DHL in the region responded incredibly well, and as a result we doubled the margin and managed to grow the business by over 50 per cent in just two years, well ahead of market growth. I learned the simple lesson that the power of full engagement can be immense: when people enjoy working for an organisation and know the organisation genuinely cares about them, they are prepared to give a heck of a lot more – it's almost like this knowledge removes the constraints on what they're prepared to do in their work. This is a message that I've emphasised throughout my career, because it's dedication like this that epitomises the role that every one of our 100,000 employees can play in the success of DHL Express. 'Sick to the stomach' has become a signature phrase within our organisation. If people don't feel that level of disappointment when they let down a customer, they shouldn't work at DHL. We even demonstrated this message in an entertaining way by giving out sick bags at a recent management conference, and suggesting that people might want to use them if they feel that they've let down a customer.

During my time in the region, it felt like EEMEA represented 'the real DHL'. It was a challenging but exciting time for several reasons: each country was entrepreneurial. The geography of the area was huge. And we were the market leaders. The quality of service we offered was the best in the region and we were getting even better with every month.

The EEMEA region comprises a massive 88 countries in total, and includes a huge diversity that ranges from Russia (the largest in the region) to Mali (the smallest). Despite its dramatic cultural diversity, we achieved a remarkable amount of social cohesion, camaraderie and harmony in the workforce. When people came together from their various countries, the only two colours that mattered to anyone were the red and yellow of DHL. My time in EEMEA proved to me that what brings us together is far stronger than what drives us apart and that a meaningful common purpose is the ulti-mate social glue. When businesses are run well, people are able to rise above any differences, and if you give them the incentives, they will do well in order to prove themselves.

Seeing how well people responded to the right sort of motivation and how seamlessly they worked together became a catalyst that enhanced all my future thinking on leadership. I'm convinced that the talent is always there – it just needs to be unlocked. We liberated people by removing the bureaucracy around them, and it amazed me how fast people were able to rid themselves of a negative mindset if you simply give them reasons to believe in the company. Peter Drucker was right when he coined the phrase 'Culture eats strategy for breakfast'. If you create the right environment for people, you will be rewarded with high performance from them.

DHL has always adopted a non-political approach to business. We strive to be compliant with international business standards, even when countries in which we operate engage in business practices that we don't find acceptable. Our unique strengths are our local presence and our knowledge of local conditions. We have a greater awareness of the local realities than anyone else, which allows us to be flexible. Our competitors often use third parties and agents, but we always use our own people. Every Country Manager is charged with building deep relationships at a governmental level, and whenever new regulations are announced, we're always the first to adopt and implement them. Whatever the difficulties or complexities of the marketplace, we're always better positioned to master them.

In addition to all this, we have a proud history of being the first to enter countries and the last to leave. As a company we are known for sticking by our customers through good times and bad. Some institutions have criticised us for operating in certain areas – I can see why they might, but our response is, and always has been, that as long as we're allowed to ship there legally and our customers want us to, we will operate there, which is what global organisations such as the United Nations and the World Bank are paying us to do. We always follow the law and we always endeavour to be where we need to be, which is where our customers are. We don't believe that it helps anyone to shut down operations or apply sanctions: when this happens, it's always the poorest people who suffer the most. After all, a big part of doing the right thing is doing it under difficult circumstances. A change of government or even a war in a country where we operate doesn't make any difference to the needs of our customers and their desire to continue their lives or their businesses. We're willing to make the investment in sustaining our unparalleled network, especially when the going gets tough. We're at our best when things are at their worst. We don't want to see any piece of our network taken out.

Nour Suliman, current CEO of DHL in the Middle East and North Africa, has been with DHL Express for 40 years. I've been working with him since 1985, and thought it would be useful if I included some words from him about how we operate in his region. Here's how he describes the secret behind DHL Express's success:

> *Today, almost 90 per cent of jobs in the Middle East are done by locals. Before Ken, expats would be considered for the key roles. Ken understands the power of local contacts and knowledge operating within a global network. People ask how it's possible for DHL to deliver to Iraq, Yemen, Syria, Libya and Iran. We say it's because we have local people there and it's our responsibility to enable them and their livelihoods. We have the right people in the right place.*
>
> *It's amazing to experience the global DHL 'Kick-on' sessions, where we bring 1,200 leaders from around the world together. It's a massive investment, but I think it's the heart of our success. It's the ultimate opportunity for people to share their insights and passion with each other. There is no substitute for real, live, person-to-person contact. People leave those events feeling renewed and invigorated. Then they take those feelings back to their people. Then their people take those feelings to their customers.*

As business becomes increasingly global, there is an increased need for trusted partners at every level. No one can afford shortcuts or ill discipline, and often all it takes is one wayward move to sully a company's global reputation. I also think that it's important to localise business as much as possible – my experience has taught me that it's far easier for people who are actually based on the ground in such places as Russia, Saudi Arabia or Nigeria to engage with local authorities and anticipate problems there. It's not always clear to outsiders why local governments behave as they do, so having strong teams based there who are able to respond in real time to changes as they occur can be a tangible advantage.

Although I believe that the local element of multinational business is important, I should also emphasise the importance of a globally integrated network. At DHL we are only as strong as our weakest member, and if our office in one country isn't at the top of its game, it can have a negative effect on every other country. As we often say, 'The strength of the country is the network and the strength of the network is the country.' We take the approach that a local problem is at the same time a regional problem and also a global problem, because of the impact that it can have elsewhere. It's a classic virtuous cycle if you get it right, but it can turn into a vicious cycle if you get it wrong. We believe we need to be on top of everything, everywhere, the whole time. After all, there is no rest for the wicked – nor for those that want to be best in the world.

My time running the EEMEA region reinforced my optimism about the express logistics business and I learned that the regions that grow most quickly can change often. We saw that any of the smallest regions could become bigger, and that the smaller entities also benefit from the infrastructure around the world. We've always been open about investing in countries that others might feel have less obvious potential, having learned that investment in every country benefits every other country in the world. In terms of how DHL works, the greater our total capacity, the greater our potential volume to and from every other country. We always approach questions such as this from a holistic network point of view.

Our philosophy can be summed up in the following three words: 'continuous global growth'. We believe the world will continue to grow, and that e-commerce and technology are two of the things that are responsible for that growth. This means that on a macro level, we never worry about limiting our investment because of a possibility that growth would falter. In fact, even during the global financial crisis we believed that the world would continue to grow. I'm very excited about the future. Our business depends on global trade. People are becoming more and more connected. They're travelling further and more frequently than ever before.

There was one moment during my time working in the Middle East when it all came together for me. It was September 2007, and we had brought 300 leaders from the 88 countries in the region together to an air-conditioned tent in Bahrain. We shared stories of triumph and trauma with each other. These were DHL veterans who had kept their operations going throughout the political changes in Russia and the armed conflict of the Gulf War. One told us how DHL couriers continued to deliver to customers in the Middle East wearing gas masks and carrying the antidote to poisonous gas. Couriers would pick up shipments from outside the region, wherever flights were safe to land, then truck them to Bahrain for distribution. The team of 40 lived together on a compound and often slept in a 'safe room' with windows covered in boards to protect them from flying glass during an attack. Air-conditioning units covered with plastic stopped any potential leak of chemicals. Another told us that during the war in the Balkans, one courier (now the Country Manager for Serbia) moved 100 kg of shipments from our office in the highest tower block in the city to the relative safety of his apartment. When the conflict ended four years later, he finally delivered the documents and parcels to the addresses that still stood – to the astonishment of the recipients.

One after another, these leaders presented their results and applauded each other. The presentations were all in English, but the real common denominator was the pride in being the best. Being part of DHL meant being part of a world-class brand that demanded everything they had and then some.

In that moment, all I was able to think about was how quickly people can shine when you give them the capability and the appreciation. Their passion for customer service was palpable. They achieve extraordinary results in conditions that are unthinkable in first-world environments. Whether it's war or regime change or earthquakes, they just step up and do it.

It was during my time in EEMEA that I first came into contact with an amazing advertising and marketing agency called Maverick. As their name suggests, they are bold and innovative and challenging the status quo. We had been working with them since 2003 on some great sales campaigns such as Reactivator (analysing dormant accounts and finding ways to get them shipping again; it was based on a *Terminator* theme, 'I'll be back'). I used them to design and promote some of my kick-off meetings such as Pole Position (positioning us as the number one on the grid but still with the race ahead), and Top Gear, where I took part in some parkour activities to show I was fit to lead.

They are still with us today, constantly innovating and coming up with fresh ideas – like a custom-designed truck interior to roll out First Choice (our in-house quality system) around the region. It was Maverick that helped design the concept of CIS and have constantly helped us build relationships with our sponsorships to drive maximum commercial value. Our relationship has lasted more than 15 years and is still as strong as ever. Today, they help drive our social media activities and our digital presence to build ever-closer relationships through e-commerce.

As I have already said, the front line is the key to the bottom line, and my time in this region bears testimony to that – in 2006, revenue was growing at a healthy 14 per cent and in 2008 it was growing at 23 per cent. The margin of earnings before interest and tax (EBIT) went from 10.5 per cent in 2006 to 20.2 per cent in 2008. Our financial success seemed counter-intuitive to some; by not placing the primary emphasis on cost reduction, as my predecessors had done, we doubled the margin. We invested in bringing people together, sharing our agenda with them and reaffirming their value to the organisation. I let them know that I trusted them to run the business, which set them free to be their best, and the results were spectacular. My performance here also put paid to the idea that I was just a 'turnaround specialist', as I had been branded by some people, rather than a leader who could take a business from good to great.

KEY LEARNING

- Make it a great place to work and people will give you a lot more.
- If you create the right environment, you will get high performance.
- A local problem is a regional problem and also a global problem.
- There is no rest for the wicked – nor for those who want to be best in the world.

CHAPTER 6:
BUSINESS IS A
CONTACT SPORT
USA 2007-2008

When you are going through hell, keep going.
This is no place to stop and rest.

Anon

Throughout my time working in Canada and EEMEA, DHL's problems in the United States were a mounting worry to the Deutsche Post board. The integration with Airborne Express, a delivery company acquired by DHL in 2003, was a complete disaster – the losses were mind-boggling, and they kept escalating. No matter how well we did elsewhere in the world, the profits were completely absorbed by the losses of our American operation.

In the American market, one of the main problems was the fact that we were taking on two of the world's fiercest and most formidable competitors, UPS and FedEx, in their own backyard. We didn't offer superior value, we didn't have demonstrable competitive advantages and we didn't have an internal infrastructure that enabled us to function with anything near efficiency – looking back on it now, it seems obvious that we were blinded by hubris, naivety and sheer incompetence. Our strength was in international rather than domestic logistics, but we somehow believed that we could build

A Yorkshireman's guide to fashion.

My sister. This guarantees my place in heaven.

My lucky day, 6 July 1989.

First in and last out in every country around the world - DHL in Bahrain 1991.

A young top gun in the Middle East, 1990.

Quality pioneers – winning the Dubai Quality Award in 1992, with Casper Weinberger (second from right).

Adrian Dalsey, Larry Hillblom and Robert Lynn at the 25th reunion.

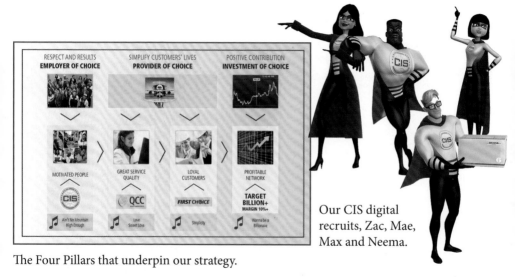

The Four Pillars that underpin our strategy.

Our CIS digital recruits, Zac, Mae, Max and Neema.

Our FOCUS strategy, ten years on and still going strong.

The Greatest International Express Company in the World

'The Speed Of Yellow' – our biggest global campaign from 2011.

The non-German German turnaround manager of the year. © Handelsblatt GmbH.

Leipzig, our European hub and the biggest of its kind in the world.

Our CIS superheroes weren't just animated.

Leading from the front as a CIS Facilitator, 2010.

Supporting Australian and New Zealander lifesavers for over 20 years.

Out with a courier, delivering e-comm in China.

From store to your door –
DHL's end-to-end
e-commerce strategy.

Endorsement from the top – me and my mum meet the Pope.

Sir Alex and Ken, Manchester United v Leeds.

Even our CIS training and engagement programme was award-winning at the *Training Journal* Awards.

Ryan Hunter-Reay in a sea of yellow – Indianapolis 500, 2014.

Founding partners of Formula E.

The fastest lap meets the fastest delivery chap.

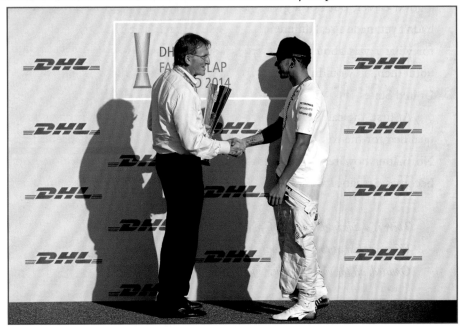

a world-class domestic operation in the United States that could compete with UPS and FedEx. It was completely unrealistic, and we got our head handed to us.

Towards the end of 2007, DHL US was losing over $100 million each month – the business was going down in flames and taking the rest of the global operation down with it. By the start of the global financial slowdown, the situation looked really dire. So much money had been sunk into the US business that people were making absurd rationalisations for the situation: I'll never forget when the loss for one month was US$113 million, but the management team was proud because the budgeted loss had been US$116 million – they treated the difference as if it was a profit! The situation taught me the danger of collective self-delusion, where no one is prepared to declare that the emperor has no clothes.

In the face of impending doom, the senior leadership of Deutsche Post decided that they needed to take drastic action. They needed someone both experienced and crazy enough to take on the assignment, and had decided that that someone was me. In September 2007, I got the call from the DHL Express global CEO to take over the United States.

I was 52 years old at the time. I had been with DHL for a quarter of a century and had done well. If I'd retired at that point, it would have been a good career, but not a great one. I had made all the right moves, but I hadn't yet made a real difference – it was as if it had all been a dress rehearsal for what I was about to do. I knew that no matter how well I had done until then, it wouldn't matter if I couldn't salvage the situation in the United States.

At first, the call came as a surprise. In retrospect, I was the person best qualified for the role but a challenge that big always takes your breath away. No matter how ready you think you are, you're still taken aback when it becomes a reality. I was reminded of Shakespeare's quote from *Julius Caesar*:

There is a tide in the affairs of men,
Which, taken at the flood, leads on to fortune;
Omitted, all the voyage of their life

Is bound in shallows and in miseries.
On such a full sea are we now afloat,
And we must take the current when it serves
Or lose our ventures.
    IV/iii/218–224

It quickly became obvious that the situation was going to require much more than just incremental changes. A succession of people had been brought in to turn around the situation, but to no avail; they had all tried to do more of the same – just better. It's easy to rationalise a soft course of action when the alternative is really hard, but it could easily have brought down the whole of Deutsche Post if it had continued for much longer. The reasons for the business's failure wasn't always apparent to the people who were brought in, and the more people arrived, the less they seemed to know about the realities of the US domestic business. The one thing that I knew was that radical action was required.

The reason that I was selected to take on this 'mission impossible' was my success in Canada – although it had been on a much smaller scale than the United States, it involved similar challenges, and there was also a realisation that no one else could do it. I don't say that as a boast; I say it because I was a last resort, the only thing that stood between DHL and the abyss.

I'd been given the job of a lifetime and knew that I had to make it work, but I also felt a sense of responsibility to turn things around. As a leader of DHL, I felt indignant that the problem had been allowed to go on for such a long time; instead of asking, 'Why me?' I thought, 'Why not me?' I knew that it was going to be tough and that there would be huge calls to make, but I was driven by a sense of duty to the company and an obligation to my colleagues and couldn't afford to doubt myself. I knew we would succeed – we just had to work out how. Looking back, I realise that it was this total certainty in the face of uncertainty that enabled my success. Not only was failure not an option, even *thinking* about failure wasn't an option!

I spent my first two months in the job surveying the American business and talking to as many DHL staff as possible, especially on the front line.

This sent a powerful message – until then, no one had made the effort to understand what it was really like for the workers on the ground. The expansion of DHL into the United States through acquisitions such as that of Airborne Express had been a feasible strategy on paper, but it had been badly executed. At the same time, DHL had attempted to build a ground operation that would compete with UPS and FedEx, making massive investment in hub facilities on both the east and west coasts. In hindsight, it's hard to believe that any company could have been so bold and blind at the same time.

I resolved to fix the situation instead of kicking the can down the road. There were those in the company who believed that things might improve without a radical change in direction, but I knew things would only get worse – money was being spent without a clear vision of what it was supposed to achieve and we lacked an inner core of people who truly knew the business or the environment, which was in striking contrast with UPS and FedEx. Even the DHL advertising campaigns were facetious, poking fun at the competition without promising anything better. We didn't stand a chance, no matter how much money we threw at the problem.

We set the standard by which all others were judged all around the world, but in the US we were a textbook example of how to do everything wrong. I remember thinking that I could sympathise with how Napoleon must have felt when he invaded Russia – the sheer vastness of the territory was insurmountable. In my first few weeks in the job, I found out that people weren't telling the truth about the situation – they weren't intentionally lying but they didn't understand what was really going on, and our underlying IT and customer service platforms were dysfunctional and unreliable. It was hard to identify where the potential problems were; the P&L (profit and loss) account was a sea of red.

Another huge problem was the fact that we were trying to build a ground network at a time when the express network was in massive decline and losing more money every month; meanwhile, our business between the US and the international market was largely ignored because it represented such a small portion of the total revenue, even though it was an essential part of the global network.

Our only means of competing was on price, so we'd reduced our prices to the point where they wasn't even covering our costs – but this meant that the more volume we generated, the more money we lost. We were also employing so many outside consultants that when I walked around the offices, I didn't recognise most of the people there, which meant that the core problems were buried in confusion. New products were being launched that didn't add value and just added to our cost – one big idea was to ship products to a US Postal Service address and delegate the final delivery of the package to them, but it just didn't work.

Good people were coming to work every day and doing what they could, but the underlying strategy guiding the business was so flawed that even the most basic levels of performance were out of reach. I didn't feel that the leadership in the US was driven by a sense of urgency. I remember saying to my colleagues at the end of one 14-hour day, 'We've worked like dogs today and have lost $4–5 million. And we'll do the same tomorrow, and the day after that.' But there was no sense of panic, because it was felt that Deutsche Post was an infinite reservoir of funds. The real insanity was that most people there couldn't see how bad the situation was. Big decisions were being made because of consultant-speak and unreliable data – no one with a practical knowledge of the business would ever have believed that it could succeed.

It's only when there is an effective master plan that people can focus on taking the right actions – in such a dire situation, anything less than radical change is futile. I needed every insight that I had learned in my 25 years at DHL to engineer a miracle, because it seemed like only a miracle could save us.

After about four months in the job, I was ready to make some big changes. I cut the board in half and brought in big talent – people like Charlie Dobbie, who was head of global operations and became my right-hand man. Most dramatically, I decided that we needed to leave the domestic express business in the United States, while still maintaining a presence in the country so as not to affect our international business. Acknowledging that we didn't need to be everywhere in order to serve international customers would enable us to save huge amounts of money.

When I first talked to Charlie about my decision, he asked who knew about it. 'You and me', I told him. We realised that we would encounter resistance from other leaders within DHL; that distraction would delay our execution of the plan for four months, but it wouldn't delay it forever. Eventually, everyone came around, and resources and people were dedicated to executing the plan – it finally felt like we were moving in the right direction.

I think it also helped us that the financial crisis was looming. The economy was slowing down measurably. We were driven by a sense of urgency that was previously lacking. If a 'burning platform' is a great way to instil momentum into a business, ours was as hot as it gets. In some ways, when you set deadlines that are ambitious but achievable, it's easier to get things done. The countdown to the 'last day' accelerates everyone's actions. I made it clear, there was no day after the 'last day'. Crises make things crystal. There is no room for ambiguity.

Charlie Dobbie was my wingman in turning around the US. He describes the experience:

When Ken was made CEO of the US, I received a call from him. It was a Sunday and I was barbecuing sausages for my kids. He mentioned to me that he 'needed a bit of help'. When I asked him, 'With what?' he told me that he was going to shut down US domestic. At the time, this was a massive statement to make because of the huge investment that had been made in building a domestic network.

He told me that he wanted me to introduce the same systems in the US that I introduced in Asia because they worked. I discovered that when Ken decides something, he immediately sets about executing it. He just goes for it. He finds the people he needs to get the job done. I don't think anyone in DHL could have turned the US around except him. Like Ken, I don't care too much about politics. I care about getting results. That's what we did.

While he shut down US domestic operations, Ken was also adamant about retaining a presence for our international business. Ken convinced the global board that 'you cannot be an international global player without having a presence in the US'.

Ken's ability to boil complex issues down into the real kernel of truth is a great skill. There were dark days during the US turnaround. I remember one night at the Renaissance Hotel in Fort Lauderdale that had become our second home. I told Ken I thought we were going through hell. And Ken replied, 'Yes, Charlie, but if you're going through hell, keep going'.

I remember that defining meeting in Cincinnati in November 2007 when we told 350 managers that they would have to tell 80 per cent of their staff that they would lose their jobs in the next year. Over the next few days, we expected all hell to break loose. But the opposite happened – business continued as usual. We never lost one day to strike or industrial action as a result of that announcement. That was a huge moment for both Ken and me. That's when I believed we had a chance of surviving the US shutdown.

I think most people in the US knew we were under massive financial pressure. I think they knew the situation was untenable. They also appreciated Ken's honesty and a clear path forward – no matter how painful it was. People also had amazing goodwill towards DHL in general. They wanted it to survive – maybe as a counter to FedEx and UPS.

Ken is prepared to make bold moves in the face of sceptics. He makes them and explains them with clarity. He is able to handle the politics inside and outside the organisation. He is able to marshal a far-flung company behind a singular purpose.

Turning around the US was a huge job. There were so many vendor agreements that had to be terminated to get back to the profitable core – from air service agreements to union agreements with the Teamsters to ground service agreements. People in Washington DC were also upset with the company for rationalising its operations – especially in an election year. The acquisition of Airborne followed by a bad integration followed by an unprofitable ground-service operation built up a big mess that was linked to the domestic market. Ken pushed forward with his team and got the job done with remarkable speed. In the process, he found the managers that would take DHL to the next level because everyone got tested in that fast-paced environment.

I remember sitting with Ken when he looked at a 'density map' indicating where the international business was originating and terminating in the US

versus where the company's footprint had evolved to. What was clear to him was
that he didn't need to be everywhere in order to serve international customers.
That enabled him to rationalise the network by 80 per cent and save huge
amounts of money.

Together with my team, I confronted the brutal reality of how we might close down a business that employed over 12,000 people across the United States, in the face of a softening economy. Because it was an election year we were exposed to particular scrutiny, but once the plan had been formulated and communicated clearly, they performed exactly as I knew they could. Within six months, we had closed down our domestic network and let go of some 9,500 people. Despite this, we executed the plan superbly, and I believe our achievements were unprecedented – we kept our international customers on board and persuaded our partners to support us.

By the end of 2007, I was physically exhausted. I had been travelling constantly and the pressure was immense – I felt the strain of letting so many people go and knew that we had a very short window to achieve our plan. We had developed a group of leaders who saw what needed to be done and then did it – there was no room for hesitation or ambivalence.

A key moment occurred during the final weekend of November 2007, when we brought 350 leaders together to our hub in Cincinnati. We began the programme with a video: a slowing heartbeat that eventually stopped beating altogether. My aim was to reinforce the idea that if we didn't act decisively, we were facing extinction. People were shocked and moved, and when I stood up to speak, you could have heard a pin drop. I then clearly communicated my vision of withdrawing from the domestic business and becoming the 'global international specialist'. I showed the extent of the financial haemorrhaging, as well as its consequences. I could see the surprise on the faces of my audience – people had known it was bad, but they didn't know just how bad. But they were also animated by the challenge in front of them – they knew what was expected of them and they were ready to execute it, even though many of them were aware that they might lose their jobs.

The plan was to provide strong leadership and end the procrastination; this commitment was strengthened by the feedback from domestic leaders when we sent them to DHL's international hubs around the world. Many of them were blinkered by a domestic mindset, but seeing how strong the company was outside America inspired them to embrace the change. They saw what being a champion really meant, and understood the power and strength of the DHL brand. They came back transformed and became passionate promoters of the cause overnight, transferring this passion and insights to their teams.

Mike Parra, CEO of DHL Americas, has some interesting thoughts about how we achieved the transformation. He says:

When I first met Ken, I was struck by his extremely high energy and passion. He seemed very focused on operational excellence. He also seemed humble. Although I'm originally from Cuba and he's from Yorkshire, I saw a huge similarity in our approaches.

When Ken led the turnaround in the US, there was massive fear and uncertainty. No one knew what was going to happen to the organisation or their role within it. Ken conducted a series of town hall meetings with people across the country. I think he had already made the decision to pull out of DHL domestic in the US but he wanted to see if anyone had a better idea. In every meeting, he would ask, 'What would you do to cut our costs and reduce our losses?' Every response referenced minor cost saving that would begin to stem the losses.

What I learnt was how narrow in scope everyone's mindset was, including mine. I also saw how open-minded he was. He had seen the finish line. He was already on the other side of the forest but we couldn't see the forest through the trees.

As I introduced Ken to everyone, I remember him saying to me one afternoon, 'Mike, I need you to do me a favour. I need you to stop introducing me to people because I don't know how many of them will be part of our organisation in the next few months.' I will never forget that. I saw into his heart. I saw how much he cared for people and how much that connection meant to him.

I remember when Ken confirmed me as the Area General Manager for the western region. That's when we moved into the next phase of the process to lay off 9,500 people. At the board meetings, Ken would share that we were now part of an international company. We needed to break the cycle of only thinking like a domestic company. He told us that we needed to understand the power of the global network. He said that the global network was also behind us – that's why we couldn't fail.

One of the most remarkable learning experiences of my career was when Ken sent me, along with a select group of my peers, around the world to visit DHL facilities and operations. I came back knowing what 'the right way' looked like. I also saw the commitment of champions outside the US to help us win. Person after person asked me a single question, 'How can we help you be successful?' There was no judgement, just the determination to strengthen a key part of the network. I also now knew who to call to get things done.

Soon after that, we met in one of our old IT facilities in Arizona and made the decision on letting go of 5,000 people. The discussion was detailed and disciplined. HR was present as we reviewed every case. Each of the four managers was responsible for letting go of approximately 1,250 people. We had to numb our feelings and just do what had to be done. We had to strap on our emotional armour because we knew we would be delivering that news to so many people and their families. It was a baptism of fire for all of us. At the same time, we had to continue to motivate existing employees to bring their all to work every day, not knowing what their future held for them.

Just over two years later, Ken told me that he was making me CEO of DHL US. In my wildest dreams, I never imagined I would rise so far. As a first generation American of Cuban immigrant parents, I was amazed to be occupying this position. I was also highly appreciative of his trust in me. I assured Ken that I would never let him down. To this day, I've learnt that Ken trusts those people who are loyal to the values of the organisation and rewards them accordingly.

Ken is accessible. He's a true mentor not just to me, but to leaders throughout the organisation. He's always asking me about the competition, what I'm hearing and how I believe we can stay ahead of them. In hindsight, I can also see that he was always preparing me for the next assignment. When I was appointed CEO of DHL Americas in 2016, I felt a huge sense of pride and confidence that Ken believed I could run the third-largest DHL region for him.

Instead of disappearing, DHL US would reinvent itself as the leader in international express, and everyone working at DHL would become Certified International Specialists. The response was extraordinary; people really rallied around the new direction and were relieved and inspired that we now had a simple, achievable plan. There was a visible path to success and it made a massive difference. People can rise to any challenge if you give them certainty – person after person stood up and shared their commitment to executing our new vision.

We examined what kind of network we needed to service about 85 per cent of the country and structured ourselves accordingly. We expected that we would lose at least 50 per cent of our international business once we rationalised our domestic routes, but with the quality of our service remaining high, we lost a lot less than I'd expected. Our partners worked with us to achieve our goals, and miraculously, we didn't lose any time to strikes, despite the changes that we'd asked the unions to accept – we somehow managed to get everyone to understand what we were doing. I learned that when people understand why things need to happen, they will be prepared to work with you.

As we implemented our plans and explained our strategy in intense detail, the excitement mounted – people could see that our solutions were working. We delivered against really tight deadlines, turning the situation around in record time. Then in 2009, we made the commitment to MAD, or Making a Dollar, and very quickly people began to see that profitability was a realistic goal, if we continued with modest growth and kept costs under control. That knowledge fired people up, and the results continued to improve – we finally broke even by the end of 2010. Since then, the United States has been a great inbound destination for the global network, and makes money – in fact, we've expanded our Cincinnati hub four times to accommodate increasing volume.

My experience facilitating the American turnaround taught me five important things:

1. **If a situation has been deteriorating for some time, you need to start again,** rather than just think about making incremental improvements – if the latter were possible, someone before you would have done it.

2. **You need to make fact-based not spreadsheet-based decisions,** which requires an understanding of how what you're offering in the marketplace compares with the competition. It also means having an accurate understanding of what your customers think about you and your capabilities.

3. **You cannot achieve anything on your own, and need people with deep, practical industry knowledge in order to win.** In a business like ours, it will always come down to how good you are at ground level. Theory doesn't cut it, but experience and action do.

4. **It's all about effective communication:** a lot of people talk about it, but very few actually do it. You need to share good news and bad news in real time. It seems obvious, but it can be difficult to recognise in the moment. We decided that we were going to be totally transparent in everything that we did, and it paid dividends.

5. **Great execution is a strategy all by itself.** Every time we delivered something on time, we earned credibility and kudos for the next time. It also made a big difference that I was prepared to lead from the front. Rather than hiding in my office and delegating the difficult jobs to others, I personally engaged my employees, looking them in the eye when sharing both good news and bad.

The real heroes are not the turnaround specialists – they're the people who grind out consistent growth, year after year. Those are the people who helped us turn the situation in the United States around. As Jeff Ward, partner and Global Transportation Practice Leader at A.T. Kearney has noted, in the process we were able to identify the managers that would 'take DHL to the next level, because everyone got tested in that fast-paced environment'. I may have inspired them, but they inspired me even more and exemplified the real culture of DHL. That's why I've been reluctant to acquire outside companies – there's always a risk that they'll clash with the company's culture, which is as crucial to our success as anything else.

In uncertain times simplicity is the ultimate virtue – the main thing is to maintain a focus on your main objective. I have always been good at narrowing the focus, but my experience running the US office showed me that it was a strategy that really did work. We built trust in everything we did: first we said what we would do and why we would do it, and then we did it. I think people realised that our decision to rationalise our domestic presence was inevitable. Even though we had invested over $2 billion and lost another $2 billion in the US, we decided that it was time to bite the bullet and cut our losses.

I·didn't think it could get any bigger or better than my American assignment, but it turned out that my time there had been preparing me for something much, much larger: the world.

KEY LEARNING

- Instead of asking, 'Why me?' ask, 'Why not me?'
- People can rise to any challenge if you give them direction and tools.
- When people understand *why* things need to happen, they will work with you on *how* things need to happen.
- When a situation has been deteriorating for some time, you need to start afresh.
- The real heroes are not the turnaround specialists – the heroes are the people who grind out consistent growth, year after year.

CHAPTER 7:
CREATING THE ORIGINAL LOCAL GLOBAL COMPANY
BECOMING GLOBAL CEO 2009

Simplicity is the most difficult thing to secure in the world;
It is the last limit of experience and the last effort of genius.
George Sand, *Letters of George Sand*

The real miracle in what we achieved in the United States was the number of customers who stuck with us through the transition. We feared that there might be a mass exodus, but in the end only a minority of our customers left us for our competitors. And importantly, the ones who stayed with us were the right ones: those who understood our strategy and valued our international expertise. The truth was that we now had something to say: we had a clearly defined proposition as a specialist in international shipping that would help facilitate our customers' global commerce. We had discovered our mission and were now out to prove ourselves to the world.

I received the call to become global CEO in January 2009. It happened while I was in Bonn, Germany. Frank Appel, CEO of Deutsche Post, called me into his office and told me that the incumbent CEO was leaving the company. I liked and respected the outgoing CEO and appreciated the support that he had always provided me. He was a big thinker who enjoyed the challenge of running a multinational business, as well as a brilliant businessman who had made his mark, and his ability and global network would ensure that he prospered whatever he did next. But now it was time for me to take the lessons we had learned in the United States and ship them worldwide.

I am an executor and, like any mature leader, I'm able to see the big picture. But, unlike most mature leaders, I'm at my best focusing on the front line. No matter how successful I become, I will always be a blunt, straight-talking Yorkshireman, and I'll always be on the side of the working class – the people who do the actual work, not the people who sit around and talk about it. One of my favourite quotes is from Teddy Roosevelt, who said:

> *It is not the critic who counts; not the man who points out how the strong man stumbles, or where the doer of deeds could have done them better. The credit belongs to the man who is actually in the arena, whose face is marred by dust and sweat and blood; who strives valiantly; who errs, who comes short again and again, because there is no effort without error and shortcoming; but who does actually strive to do the deeds; who knows great enthusiasm, the great devotions; who spends himself in a worthy cause, who at the best knows in the end triumph of high achievement and who at the worst, if he fails, at least he fails while daring greatly. So that his place shall never be with those cold and timid souls who know neither victory nor defeat.*

I had no doubt that I could build the greatest international company in the world, because I had seen where the company could go and believed that I had the ability to help it get there. In fact, I specifically remember thinking, 'I'm built for this. This is my time to help this company become the best in the world'.

As I've already said, I never set the goal of becoming the global CEO; I've simply answered the call to the best of my ability each time I was asked to. And even when I was offered the top job, some people still said I was only a good turnaround expert, and doubted I could grow a business for the long term. That just proves you have to keep proving yourself.

If you expect great things from people and you give them the freedom to achieve them, they will rise to your level of expectation. The real secret of leadership is convincing people to believe in themselves and then to fully express their talent. It's about achieving bottom-line targets while helping people achieve their most important goals; in fact, these two goals must be indistinguishable, and they were certainly fused in my mind. By making me global CEO, Frank Appel had clearly demonstrated that he had the greatest confidence in me. I also possessed the autonomy to pursue the course of action that I believed was best for the company. At the time, DHL was just limping along; even though we were making good progress in the United States, we were still not completely out of the woods. Even the European business that was supposed to be our stronghold was only budgeted to break even.

In one way, there is a great freedom in taking over a business that is struggling. Unlike when you take charge of a highly profitable enterprise, you have to act quickly and decisively rather than taking the traditional 100 days to review the situation. You're not just there as a caretaker; you're there as an agent of change and have the latitude to apply your vision of the future. DHL was 40 years old in 2009, and it was time for the company to finally grow up and achieve the two most important priorities of any corporate adult: firstly, to create and retain customers, as Peter Drucker says. And secondly, to make money.

Although the task looked like a gargantuan one, I believed that I knew exactly what needed to be done to turn the global operation around. Despite the adverse global economic conditions and some big losses, I could see the depth and breadth of potential that was just waiting to be unleashed. Even though I was surrounded by fear and anxiety, I was confident in the Big Yellow Machine's capacity to kick into gear. It was just a matter of time. Europe was our largest region, comprising two-thirds of our global business. It soon became apparent to me that a lot of the problems here were being caused by their domestic businesses – it was like the problems we had faced in the United States, all over again.

The situation was made harder by the fact that in 2009, DHL faced massive economic headwinds, along with the rest of the world. All the external economic indicators were negative and the global financial crisis was still intensifying. Governments and businesses around the world had been confronted with what the scholar and former trader Nassim Nicholas Taleb calls a 'Black Swan'. This is a once-in-a-generation event that no one predicted could be possible but that changes everything when it happens, and we were still coming to terms with it. It was against this difficult backdrop of worldwide distress that I charted the forward course for the company.

Although we had stabilised the situation in the US, we would still lose €700 million that year. In the absence of external positive indicators, we had to find the motivation that would allow us to jump-start our recovery. My first priority was to ensure that all my colleagues shared my optimistic view of our future; they had to see the growth and success that would come after the temporary economic decline that we were experiencing. I knew that we were in an industry that would continue to grow, and our challenge was to grow faster than the industry.

The good news was that people in the company were just waiting to act. Like in the US, they wanted a clear plan that would enable them to move forwards rather than sideways, which is what they'd been doing for so long had felt like. Over the next few months, I wrote a five-year plan that explicitly outlined our goals and our strategy. It was definitely ambitious but still felt achievable. It laid out our key deliverables for each year as follows:

Earnings before Interest and Taxes

		EBIT Target €	EBIT Achieved €
2010	Stabilise the business	500 million	497 million
2011	Invest and prepare for growth	900 million	916 million
2012	Grow our market share	1 billion	1.1 billion
2013	Become a provider of choice	1.1 billion	1.1 billion
2014	Become an employer of choice	1.3 billion	1.3 billion
2015	Become an investment of choice	1.5 billion	1.4 billion

Each one of our revenue targets was substantially ahead of market growth, but there's a great power in putting your goals in writing and declaring them to the world. Once I'd put my intentions out there, there was no going back. I've also learned that just giving people a plan will increase their confidence – it can feel like seeing the future in advance. It also gives people a scoreboard of success, something that they can track their performance against. Like any other plan, the closer you come to achieving it, the more confidence people will have in it. Consistency of purpose, certainty of direction and proof of achievement were going to be three critical contributory factors to our success.

We were also helped in our task by the fact that our competition, UPS and FedEx, had problems of their own in their domestic markets and had not been able to seize on the opportunity to exploit our weakness. Outside the United States, we were still number one in terms of global market share, with UPS our biggest rival in Europe and FedEx the main competition in Asia. I decided to focus on becoming the best in the world at the part of our business that was going to expand most rapidly in the foreseeable future, which was the thing that we were best at and also the thing that we had pioneered some 40 years previously: time-definite international shipping. No one else could move packages like we could across all borders and in all conditions. At the time, it represented 50 per cent of our business; today, it has grown to 70 per cent.

Our unique strength is our global outlook – we're the most international company in the world, and we also invented the industry. We needed to put all our efforts into maintaining this lead. As I had risen towards the top of the company, I'd always felt that it was geographically fractured – the various regional offices felt separate from each other, which undermined the idea that we were one company. We had built separate businesses in Europe, the Middle East, the Americas, Africa and Asia, which meant that our organisation was naturally decentralised, but also inherently fragmented. Not only did one hand not know what the other did – it didn't even care. We had a great spirit but there was no one at the top to bring it all together, which had led to the company being unmanageable and unprofitable. Deutsche Post's focus on growing domestic capacity also took DHL away from its roots as an international specialist and contributed to the company's decline.

I'd been a DHL manager in some of the most challenging countries in the world – places such as Yemen. As I drilled down into the company's challenges, I knew I was the right person for the global CEO job, because I'd held a range of different roles and had proven that I knew the business. I knew we had to establish a global strategy and establish a leadership team that was embraced by the countries. We had to become a network of people truly committed to a common cause. If we wanted to be the best international express logistics company in the world, everybody who worked for us needed to be terrific at their job. It wasn't a case of hiring only people who were especially gifted; we needed to inspire ordinary people to be extraordinary. I felt like living proof of what could be achieved with a clear idea of *what* was expected and *how* to achieve it. I hadn't ever wanted a central 'command-and-control' model; I wanted a 'commit-and-communicate' model, where everyone was inspired to perform at the highest level.

'As one' had become the rallying cry that I introduced to save the United States business, and when I got the global job, my key message was that I wanted to get staff all over the globe working as one. I made it clear that if we were at all fractured, the turnaround might not work. We could succeed if we saw the whole world as a network, and the only bottom line that mattered to us should be the bottom line of the entire company. For example, even though it was more expensive to drive sales in the United States, we had to grow there, because it reduced the cost of the global business and increased its quality, which resulted in the high level of profits that we enjoy today. Our 'network mentality' would be our secret weapon and we knew that together, we could overcome each other's weaknesses. I wanted us to get into a virtuous cycle where everybody trusted the leadership to make the right decisions for our customers, shareholders and employees.

I was also keen to build company activities relating to social responsibility, because it's an integral part of connecting people and improving lives. I wanted people to see how excited we were to do things for each other and the world. My message was 'Be proud of your function, be proud of your country, be proud of your region, and most importantly, be proud of your network – because that's where all of our success eventually comes from'.

The world is increasingly more relevant in business. The e-commerce revolution is linking together everyone, everywhere. Despite the nationalistic rhetoric emanating from leaders in certain parts of the world, the trend towards global integration is increasing, and it's here to stay.

One of the most important philosophies that I introduced after becoming global CEO was the idea that we could be global by being local, everywhere. And this is where the importance of trust really came in. I needed to trust an Asian to run the Asian part of the business, a Middle Easterner to run the Middle East part of the business and an American to run the American part of the business. In the past, we used mainly expats to run the regions, but I took this leap of faith, though it wasn't a leap at all – it was the right thing to do. Since taking on the global CEO job, I have had to really trust people to get things done, and I've very rarely been disappointed. They also trust me to have their backs; it's reciprocal, and trust is the ultimate binding factor.

Our strength is in our local knowledge and presence, combined with an essential entrepreneurial nature that goes all the way back to the very roots of DHL. We were never overcapitalised, which meant that we always had to look for the most ingenious way to solve a problem or exploit an opportunity. We trust in our history, and we are 'the original local global company'. One of our strengths is the fact that we look like an Australian company in Australia, a South African company in South Africa and a Chinese company in China.

Ken Lee, CEO of DHL Express Asia Pacific, has some interesting thoughts on the issue of our internationalist outlook:

I first met Ken when he was CFO of Asia Pacific. Immediately, he struck me as someone guided by a very simple philosophy: find out what works and what doesn't work. Do what works.

I remember Ken making a presentation in a sales meeting. He stuck some envelopes filled with cash under random seats. During his presentation, he asked all the salespeople to stand up and look under their seats. To their surprise, some found the cash and were allowed to keep it. Ken shared the moral of the story: you have to get off your ass to make money!

Ken shared with me that every Country Manager should spend at least 70 per cent of his time in the field. You won't find opportunities just sitting behind your desk.

In big companies, leaders can become fixated on their own silos and KPIs (key performance indicators). Ken ensures that leaders are focused on the issues that impact the network as a whole. If things don't work, we get rid of them and move on.

Ken's laser-like focus on the fundamentals has made the difference. 'Transforming while performing' has been our goal – we do best in operating mode while we transform into what we want to be.

Back in 2009, Ken Allen was very clear: we have to turn this company around. And the best way to do that is focus on selling one kind of product: cross-border time-definite international (TDI) shipping. Often, the best ways to do things are the simplest. Ken stripped away everything that got in the way of becoming the best international express company in the world.

Ken Allen has never been a fan of centralisation. He has also believed in disseminating authority to the countries and the network. Creating centralised roles multiplies more roles to serve the centralised role. One ends up doing many things that don't make customers or shareholders happy.

One of the most meaningful things that Ken did was encourage us never to have 'meetings without scrutiny'. By that, he meant that senior managers often set up meetings that rob their people of precious time without adding value to the business. Meetings that achieve nothing are the bane of front-line people's lives. It's all about only doing things that sell more noodles, make more money, pay more bonuses.

If Ken Allen wasn't the CEO, I don't even know if DHL would be run by an Asian. Asia only began to be run by an Asian when Ken became CEO. It seems so natural now. But before Ken took over, there was a philosophy that 'whatever is made in the West is the best'. Today, over 80 per cent of the Asian management board is Asian. That is a testimony to Ken's ability to adapt the business to the local culture.

Even though Ken sings and dances on the stage, I think he is a very reflective leader. He takes time to process information before he makes key decisions. Once he makes the decisions, he acts fast. The fun of working with Ken is that what he wants is crystal clear.

Ken Allen's story may not have been possible at any other company. Last year I shared a message with my region: success without celebration is not enjoyment. If people help the company succeed but they don't benefit directly, they are not going to keep giving their best to the company. Whenever Ken sees great results from a country in a business review, he always asks the question: are we rewarding our people enough? Not matter how process driven we are, we are also dealing with people. We have to make sure they get the return they deserve through their hard work.

People enjoy working at DHL because their success is celebrated and recognised. It comes from the top. Ken listens to the floor. In his heart, he's a front-line kind of guy.

I've been with DHL for 21 years. I've come up through the ranks to become a regional CEO. Over the past ten years, we have been consistent in what we want to achieve. We've gone from Focus 2010 to Focus 2020. Sometimes, the most difficult things to achieve are the easiest: be consistent, keep it simple. We continue to drive TDI. We want to invest every one of our 100,000 people around the world with passion for TDI.

At a recent global board meeting, I told Ken that my son was calling DHL a dinosaur because he said that millennials like to engage with services through a mobile app, not calling customer service. They are our customers and employees of the future. Ken listened. We now have DHL mobile apps. I don't have to pull my punches with him. I can always tell him what's on my mind.

Someone once asked me what it's like to work for a German company. I responded by saying that if I didn't know DHL was owned by Deutsche Post, I wouldn't know that it's a German company. DHL Express is first and foremost an international company.

Employing local people in local roles has made a huge difference to the organisation. I don't think our Regional Managers would have risen to the top if I hadn't become global CEO and pushed this local agenda in the way I have. These people can thereafter be role models; it's something of a virtuous cycle, and it allows us to raise the performance of every person in the organisation when they want to create something special.

With regards to Frank Appel, as I mentioned earlier, I respected him for giving me the job – it was my chance to do something and he knew I would have to apply radical surgery to remake DHL. He put his trust in me when he could have gone outside the business. In that sense, it was a courageous decision and if he hadn't taken it, I wouldn't have had the chance to do what I did. When you've had great success, it's easy to succumb to the temptation of being good, because you lose your appetite for risk or making the hard calls. I needed to sustain the hunger and drive that had been automatic in my earlier years. Over the decades, I'd evolved from the aggressive 'young buck' to a more discerning, prudent elder statesman. My sharp edges had been softened, but I still wanted to hold people accountable for taking action and doing their jobs. I didn't want to look back and dissect what went wrong; I wanted people to get it right, so we could look back and celebrate our success. Talk and hindsight are fool's errands, while action and urgency are what makes this business so great.

My willingness to bust bureaucracy and realign the company also sent a strong message to our people that we could do what's right for the future, rather than what was consistent with the past. People needed to believe in the outcome and be willing to take the appropriate action that would enable us to get there. I've always believed that you have to show results first, so the culture would follow. People have a strong drive to make things happen if they believe and trust in their leadership. In sport, when you score a goal or win the cup, the celebration is immediate. Business victories are different, because they tend to result from slow builds. The thing that thrilled me most was seeing that the members of my team were able to come together to achieve incredible results.

I had never set myself the goal of becoming the global CEO but have simply answered the call to the best of my ability every time opportunity came knocking. When I was offered the job, I felt like I had just been hired by a huge football team like Real Madrid and now had to help them win their next European Cup. I knew I had already been successful and got things done, but now I had to prove that I could turn around DHL Express – with a workforce of over 100,000 people in over 200 countries and territories. As I've already mentioned, people said that I was a good turnaround expert, but that I didn't know how to run and grow a business in the long term, which just made me even more determined to keep on proving myself. I had stopped, stepped back, reflected – and gone back to basics, applying my idea of SELF Reflection. I then wrote a simple, detailed strategic plan, and shared it widely around the company.

KEY LEARNING

- You have to show results first, so the culture can follow – results are the only true sign of excellence.
- Inspire ordinary people to be extraordinary. Give them the freedom, support and training.
- 'Commit and communicate' rather than 'command and control'.
- Focus on becoming the best in the world at your core business.
- Giving people a published plan will increase their confidence – it can feel like seeing the future in advance.

CHAPTER 8:
TIME FOR RADICAL SIMPLICITY
WELCOME TO FOCUS 2010-2020

Most strategies are like New Year's resolutions, full of really good intent but no desire or capability to execute.

Ken Allen

There is a great work by James Heskett, Earl Sasser and Leonard Schlesinger called *The Service Profit Chain*, which was first published in 1997. In a 2008 article on this seminal book entitled 'Putting the Service-Profit Chain to Work', which appeared in the *Harvard Business Review*, authors Heskett, Sasser and Schlesinger, together with Thomas Jones and Gary Loveman, wrote about the linkages between profitability, customer loyalty and employee satisfaction, and productivity.

Heskett, Sasser and Schlesinger encourage business leaders to ask a series of questions about what enables them to build world-class organisations. I took each of these to heart and they still guide my actions every day. They are

1. To what extent is the company's leadership:

- Energetic, creative versus stately, conservative?
- Participatory, caring versus removed, elitist?

- Listening, coaching and teaching versus supervising and managing?
- Motivating by mission versus motivating by fear?
- Leading by means of personally demonstrated values versus institutionalised policies?

2. How much time is spent by the organisation's leadership personally developing and maintaining a corporate culture centred on service to customers and fellow employees?

Within weeks of becoming global CEO, I had made the decision to focus on being focused. There was so much noise within the company and so much fear and uncertainty about the global financial meltdown that it felt like people were just waiting to see what would happen next. The core principle of my approach was that I wanted everything to be simple and relevant to the realities of every single person in their role at DHL. No matter who they were, I wanted it to be clear to them that they had an important role in sales and customer service.

Once again, I applied my guiding philosophy of SELF Reflection in order to really lay down what we needed to do:

SIMPLICITY

We want to build the Greatest International Express Company on the Planet. This was the simple, unifying idea – and I was confident that we would win by growing time-definite international shipping. I told everyone that we were going to concentrate on fixing our core business, which meant that we would be experts in international express only. This means that when I wake up in the morning, I'm thinking about what has happened all over the world over-night, while when my counterparts at FedEx and UPS wake up, I would guess that they're thinking primarily about the US domestic market. Our ability to maintain our international focus at DHL is what sets us apart – everything we do is seen through the lens of how we build our global network.

As I sat down to draft my plan, I considered the three questions that Jim Collins suggests that growing businesses ask themselves in *Good to Great*:

- What are we passionate about?
- What are we good at?
- What drives our economic engine?

In our case, the answer to all three questions was simple, because it was the same in each case – international express. Once I had that as an answer, the rest was easy to design. The real secret of our success lay in getting the message out there to our 100,000-strong global team. The Focus strategy gave people something to believe in and the confidence that it was achievable – providing clear direction, pragmatic realism and passionate inspiration in one go.

EXECUTION

I told everyone that we had a strategic plan for them to follow, which I called 'doing things'. To be in this company, everyone in every various function had to be the greatest in our industry. Everyone who worked for us had to be a superstar in the international express profession. Couriers needed to be the best couriers. Salespeople needed to be the best salespeople. Engineers needed to be the best engineers. Finance people needed to be the best finance people. In turn, they would attract other A-players. I made it clear that to me, execution is the result of inspiring ordinary people to do extraordinary things.

LEADERSHIP

I decided to take decisive action and halved the corporate board to just six people, surrounding myself with experts in the field who shared my passion, care and love for the business. The fact that we managed the superstars of the international express business was critical to my strategy, and I was keen that we had to treat them as such. In turn, this drove a mindset where managers had to coach and motivate rather than command and control. I wanted a united 'commit and communicate' leadership approach, where everyone was inspired and informed to perform at the highest level. That takes a special kind of leadership style and culture – one we have focused on building and embedding over the ten years since I took over the reins.

I also needed my leaders to be clear on what they had to do to make our strategy and our turnaround a reality. I launched my Focus plan at a series of regional leadership meetings around the world at the end of 2009. I concentrated everyone's attention on the big picture of growing and strengthening our position as number one in international express, but at the same time I also focused on the specific actions that I expected each of our 220 Country Managers to take. I told them that we would only be successful if every leader did what was expected of them – there was no room for uncertainty. I told them that, as a minimum, we expected:

- Personal accountability and close relationships with our top 20 customers and their senior management teams.
- Contact at national level with the customs services, in addition to other regulatory bodies.
- An expectation that all key performance indicators would be reviewed at regular intervals.
- Customs security and gateway reviews, in order that we could achieve market-leading clearance times and processes.
- Monthly formal management meetings with full functional team and service providers.
- Monthly face-to-face communication with all staff.

FOCUS

I called the overall strategy that I unveiled Focus 2010, because that's what we had to do! It established the Four Pillars that would be fundamental in supporting the DHL Express global resurgence for the next decade: Motivated People, Loyal Customers, Great Service Quality and a Profitable Network. We wanted every one of our people, no matter what their role, to be able to recite these Four Pillars and also communicate how they could help execute on helping to achieve them.

In order to create this strategy, I drew on a range of tried-and-tested insights and principles that would help to craft DHL's focus. As someone once told me, it's the way we stitch a business together that sets it apart. I knew I had to communicate our priorities at an emotional level if I wanted people to respond accordingly.

We created a vocabulary at DHL – I realised that we all speak a common language and decided to call it exactly as I saw it. From the beginning, I wanted everyone to listen to my straight talk and to know that I wouldn't hide anything from them – if I was allowed to say it, I would! I was adamant that it was important to treat every DHL employee as an equal partner in our journey towards being the best in the world. I was also conscious of communicating in a way that would connect with every employee, no matter what his or her nationality was. There was no room for subtleties or nuances – there would be no misunderstandings or confusion on my watch.

This is what I said in my address:

The Express Division as a whole has underperformed for the last nine years: this is clearly not acceptable. We are still the market leader in international express overall, but in traditional economics the market leader should have the best return. We need to focus on driving profitability in our core products.

We are in danger of losing our market leader position in international express, as we have been distracted with numerous integrations – projects not aligned to our core time-definite international shipping business and other non-value-added activities.

Market leaders remain market leaders by adapting quickly to changing circumstances, so the sensible approach is to re-evaluate our position and concentrate on core profitability. We believe that DHL's future lies in a re-emphasis on our core products, on what we're known for doing best with an unwavering focus on sales, customer service and a front-line team, free to deliver a more profitable DHL.

Clearly the time has come to take decisive action and regain lost ground. And that's why I'm asking every one of you, our global team, to read through the content of this document thoroughly and be clear in your own mind what it is we need to do now. As they say, 'a crisis is the best time for the best to play at their best'. I believe we have the best team in international express – and now's the time to prove it.

Paul Romer, a Stanford economist, once said, 'a crisis is a terrible thing to waste', advice that seemed very relevant to our situation. I had been gifted with a fantastic crisis: results that were dramatically below our capacity. It didn't matter what was going on around us – I knew that if we were able to perform at the level we were designed to perform at, we would achieve a record-breaking turnaround, which is exactly what happened.

I continued:

Here's an honest view of the current situation, and why we'll be running in operating mode. We recognise that we have issues and will be open and transparent with all problems:

- *Our ability to integrate domestic businesses – especially large ones – has been limited. We underestimated the complexity, cultural fit and IT issues involved.*
- *Where we have invested for growth in infrastructure and aviation, we are now finding it difficult to reduce costs in line with declining volumes.*
- *We have a considerable amount of overhead in high-cost locations.*
- *We focus too much on regions and not enough on countries and products.*
- *We have a weak position on North America and Canada, which we need to defend.*

With this in mind, we will continue to run our business in an operating mode over the coming years. By this, we mean making the most of what we already have: we need to maximise the utilisation of all our systems, processes and capacity. We need to use all the functionality of what we have and run it at the lowest cost possible. In financial terms, we call it 'sweating the assets' – our current infrastructure can provide excellent service and has the capacity to handle a number of years of growth. We will:

- *Invest in the business and countries that are profitable for us, investing and developing in order to increase market share, efficiency and the bottom line.*
- *Adopt an aggressive and proactive approach, driving sales productivity, efficiency and effectiveness, in order to protect our customer base and grow our market share.*
- *Make no further acquisitions, and exit from products where necessary.*
- *Abstain from commissioning any elaborate advertising campaigns; instead we will use local PR, e-marketing and other low-cost innovative approaches.*

- *Apply a strategy to identify and correct the cause of underperforming domestic businesses.*
- *Overhaul our entire structure, in order to reduce overheads.*

I wanted to hammer home the point that I was planning to jettison everything that wasn't adding value to the business or enabling us to serve our customers more effectively. I knew that if we wanted to achieve a historic turnaround, I had to instil a stripped-down, make-it-happen, zero-excess mentality. The time for carelessness was over and we were at a point where every step counted, so we needed to count every step.

Throughout my career, I had seen the waste and destruction that had been caused by the empty rhetoric of company leaders. I had witnessed the huge disconnect that frequently existed between impressively grand strategies and shocking execution. So I resolved never to formulate strategies that would satisfy only the narcissism of the top levels of management and instead resolved to make our strategy and execution one and the same thing.

As part of what we called the Focus 2010 plan, I declared publicly:

Execution is the key to a more profitable future: we have a strategic plan, it's called 'doing things'.

Execution is the tough, difficult, daily grind of making sure we are constantly improving our customer intimacy, service quality, people motivation and bottom line. It's the daily review of performance and the idea of making sure that we have the people and processes in place to out-execute our competition in the marketplace, day in and day out. Superb execution is not just about doing the right things; it's about doing the right things faster, better, more often and more productively than our competitors. This is hard work, and it is driven by a high-performance culture.

In this culture, all employees need to be committed to the success of the organisation. The products and support services are first-rate. Everyone cares about quality and should be sick to our stomachs if we disappoint even a single customer. Losing to a competitor is a blow that should make people angry. Mediocrity will not be tolerated, while excellence will be praised, cherished and rewarded. In short, business with high-performance cultures are winners, and no person of substance would want to work anywhere else. This is our goal.

Dong Ming Wu, our CEO in China, had this to say about those early days of Focus:

I first started to work with Ken when he became global CEO. He made it his mission to understand China immediately after he stepped into the role. He really understood the business but he spoke to a lot of people, not just management, to understand the most important issues. Once he formed a point of view, he searched for information to prove or disprove it. Everything that Ken does is based on the facts and he works very hard to uncover them.

One of his first decisions was to get out of China domestic operations, just like he did in the US. Ken lived in Asia for a long time so he understands the culture. He is the kind of person who also really appreciates and adapts to the local way. He would also constantly ask my advice even on small things. For example, if we were having dinner with customers or other partners, he would ask me whether he should wear a tie or take it off. He always wants to make people feel comfortable.

I've been working for DHL for 21 years. In the beginning, I don't think that DHL had a very clear strategy. Everyone seemed to be doing their own thing. There was no single priority that guided everything else. Ken was the first leader to define a clear strategy for global. It was also implementable. It was logical. It was understood by everyone from the front-line salesperson and courier to the most senior customer. That's his biggest strength: he educates and motivates everyone to commit to the strategy. He had to make a lot of tough decisions. He made them and he made them right. He demanded growth but also the right kind of profitable growth.

Ken says that 'everyone is in sales'. But Ken is also the best salesperson for DHL. Although he is not from China, people feel like they know him. There are no barriers around him. He may be the global CEO but he is also just 'Ken'. In the beginning, we weren't used to Ken's style. In China, leaders tend to be more reserved and hierarchical. But the more he told the story and linked it to music, the more they believed in him. The secret was that Ken told exactly the same story every time he came to China. He was absolutely consistent. And his approach delivered results. When people knew that he was coming to China, they smiled because they knew they would have to sing 'Ain't No Mountain High Enough'. After a while, they believed it was natural for a CEO to act like that.

Ken is a funny guy. He always tries to make people laugh but sometimes it's not easy in Asia because of the language barrier. I remember one time when my direct reports and I went out for dinner with Ken. He came up with the crazy idea that everyone had to tell a joke. They tried their best to translate Chinese humour into English. They immediately tried to use their mobile phones to Google a good joke. It didn't work for everyone but it also sent a message that people shouldn't be afraid to talk no matter how silly their words sounded. Ken showed that he appreciated and enjoyed every person's performance. Ultimately, it was a very amusing evening. People also enjoyed laughing at each other's attempt to tell the jokes in English, especially when it didn't work.

It didn't happen overnight. I think it took about three years before the Chinese really bought into Ken's message. The leaders understood that they had to become models of Ken's message. We realised that we were all Ken's ambassadors. We learned to walk the talk. People became proud of working for the most international company in the world.

China can be an insular culture. But the CIS training and the global leadership forums expanded our people's perspective. Fifty leaders went to the first global leaders meeting in Dubai in 2013. They were very excited by what they experienced. They brought that excitement back with them to China and transferred it to their people. It paid off because in 2017, China became the number one revenue and earnings generator in the network.

KEY LEARNING

- Focus on improving the core business.
- Ask the three big questions: What are we passionate about? What are we good at? What drives our economic engine?
- Doing things/execution is a strategic plan.
- Everyone is a superstar.
- Leave no room for uncertainty – specific actions.
- Create a strategy everyone can recite.

CHAPTER 9:
CONSTRUCTING THE FOUR PILLARS
IT ALL STARTS WITH MOTIVATED PEOPLE

The ability to Simplify means to eliminate the unnecessary
So that the necessary may speak.
> Hans Hofmann

My Focus 2010 strategy established the Four Pillars that would support the DHL global resurgence for the next decade. They were:

1) Motivated people – who will deliver
2) Great service quality – which will result in
3) Loyal customers – who will drive a
4) Profitable network – which will then allow us to reinvest in all of the above.

I want every person who works for DHL, no matter what their role, to be able to recite those Four Pillars and communicate how they can help execute them. We've even selected songs that celebrate each pillar – and at every meeting, I lead people in a singalong session.

WHY FOCUS ON MOTIVATED PEOPLE?

At DHL Express, we spend €1 billion on capital expenditure every year. We build great automated hubs and fantastic facilities, we fly 777 aircraft around the world, we have great IT systems that arrange the clearance of shipments while they are in the air and before they arrive at customs authorities around the world, we have a brand that is worth €15 billion, and we have amazing billing systems that allow shipments to be billed anywhere in the world and in almost any currency. Our training programmes are the most global in the world and we are proud to call ourselves the most international company in the world.

However, out of all that, what does our customer actually experience? Some of that? All of that? None of that? In truth, the only thing that the customer experiences is the courier who picks up and delivers their package and the customer service agent who takes the bookings and resolves any issues. They are the part of the company that is visible to the most important people in our business – our customers. They are our brand ambassadors, so they have to be well trained, respectful, knowledgeable and helpful, and they have to do it all from the heart, because they are a key part of our 'Insanely Customer-centric Culture'.

Imagine a shipment being picked up in Germany at 5pm, processed through our automated facilities in Leipzig, flown on a Boeing 777 aircraft to Hong Kong, cleared in 20 minutes through customs as a result of our state-of-the-art clear-in-the-air capability and out on the road for delivery at 8am the next day. Now, what if the courier delivering it to the customer was late, or rude or not adequately dressed? The result would be that all our investment would be degraded if our front line were not 100 per cent committed. So, making sure our 100,000-strong global team is motivated to ensure this never happens is our number one priority, and one we take incredibly seriously.

Our global management teams are 100 per cent committed to doing the simple things and all ensure that we have the best-trained and most motivated people in the industry. They know this is the secret to our success; it's not just something you only do when you have time, it's the main part of your job as a DHL Express leader. As well as the day-to-day engagement of our people – making sure they 'have a best day every day', we have some other simple and now institutionalised processes to ensure that we get it right when it comes to motivating our teams. Here are a few examples of what we do as a matter of course, every year in all of our 220 operating countries:

A personal favourite of mine is our appreciation weeks. Here, management teams cook a meal and serve it to the front-line staff, to say a simple 'thank you' for doing an amazing job. It's a great illustration of our belief in servant leadership. One gesture that made a huge statement was awarding €100 to every person in the company – and there are 100,000 of us in total. That was over a €10-million expense, but I felt we had to do something for the front-line people who weren't benefiting from the success of the company. €100 may not mean very much to someone earning a big salary in Europe, but it represents a couple of weeks' pay to an Ethiopian courier. This gesture helped to further build our worldwide culture and showed everyone how serious we were about looking after our employees.

We also recognise our people by giving each one a gift, whether it be Manchester United T-shirts or an invitation to a family picnic or to see Cirque du Soleil. We want our front-line staff to know that they're a huge part of our success.

We have get-togethers where our staff play football or other sports – this helps to further build the 'people network', which is just as important as the 'process network'. When we hold one of these events in Europe, we might have 3,000 front-line employees attending. These are massive events for employees, as well as their family and friends. They are professionally run and full of fun and friendly competition – it's one big party.

Our football tournaments are held annually for teams of DHL people competing for trophies in Europe, the Americas, the Middle East, sub-Saharan Africa and Asia. It all began as a small, informal kickabout in the Netherlands which rapidly grew into the EuroCup. But it's more than an excuse for people to show off their soccer and cheerleading skills. It's competitive but also inclusive and sociable, where staff members meet up with friends from across the region. For some, it may be the first time they put a face to a voice on the phone they speak with every day – and the level of camaraderie (and partying!) is off the scale.

DHL's Got Talent is an event that uncovers the fantastic talent of the great people we have working in our network. It started in the UK, leaped across the Atlantic to the Americas and has now spread to our other regions creating a huge success with employees from around the world who enter to share their unique abilities in categories including music, singing and dancing, fashion, arts and culture and of course our 'wild card' category for those talents that don't fit into a traditional category. It's a great fun event that brings the performing side out of our gifted employees and it's always uplifting to see the support and camaraderie that bring DHL together. The unique talents across our network are what make DHL the company it is today.

And hot on the heels of its success, we also launched DHL's Got Heart in 2017, a scheme to find the people who are working in their own time for a charity that's dear to their heart. We discovered that the people who did the most good for their communities were not the senior managers, but the customer service agents and couriers. They are rooted in their communities and want to do what's best for the communities – and they're exactly the kind of person I want to attract to the organisation. Participants take part in mini challenges and can win prizes and money from DHL, which they can use to help develop their own favourite charities. It's one of the most humbling things we do, because it shows the inner beauty and compassion of our people and also helps them with the causes they care most about. We want people to give their all and give something back to the communities they serve.

You'll find amazing superstars everywhere in the organisation whenever you give them the chance to shine. The more I have seen our outrageously talented and committed people around the world, the more I've realised that business plays an incredibly important role in the world and one that is quite frankly impossible for politicians to fill. Martin Luther King said, 'I have a dream', and so do we. We want DHL Express to be the best in the world at what we do *and* we want DHL Express to be an example of the 'world at its best' where we all work together. And I'm thrilled when I see that happening all around the world.

In DHL Express, we are a global family of over 100,000 people. We don't care if you're female, male or other; black, white or yellow; Catholic,

Jewish, Muslim or anything else; gay, straight or whatever. All that matters is the answer to the following question: 'Do you love our customers and your colleagues?' If the answer is yes, that's all you need.

Motivated People is characterised by the song 'Ain't No Mountain High Enough', which was written by Nickolas Ashford and Valerie Simpson and first recorded and released by Marvin Gaye and Tammi Terrell in 1967. The words might not be new but they're more relevant today than ever, and they have been perfect to drive our global resurgence. I just love this song, and every time I hear it, I feel like celebrating all over again. And after singing it a few thousand times, I can even keep the tune. Every company in the world talks about motivated people, but we wanted to find a way to get the message from the CEO to the courier or the ramp agent in real time, and nothing travels faster than the speed of music!

WHY FOCUS ON GREAT SERVICE QUALITY?

It's simple – great service quality is what we promise our customers, and it's something of an obsession for us. We have embedded great global standard operating procedures (GSOPs) that work brilliantly across the business. The result is that we can achieve a requested transit time nearly every time, 365 days a year, all around the globe. When things occasionally go wrong, it is generally because someone has not followed procedure, which results in a poor service quality for our customers. As I've said elsewhere, this makes us 'sick to our stomachs', so as part of our drive to create an 'Insanely Customer-centric Culture', we have a real focus on fixing these exceptions. And to make sure that our staff understand just how bad they should feel when things go wrong and we have to swing into service recovery, we printed our 'fix exceptions process' on a sick bag to highlight the cause and effect.

Charlie Dobbie, EVP of Global Network Operations, IT & Aviation for DHL Express, says best how seriously we take our responsibility to provide a great service:

One day I saw a consignment bag left behind by the shuttle taking the packages to the airport. Seeing it left behind made me feel physically ill that there were customer shipments that would miss the flight. I grabbed the bag and drove it to the airport myself, and it made the flight.

That single story epitomises the role that every one of our tens of thousands of people can play in the success of DHL Express.

Focusing on quality also pays big dividends. We've developed and widely shared a simple 1–10–100 rule. What we explain to everyone is that if they follow process and do their job correctly, it costs $1. If there's a mistake and we pick up the problem in the hub and have to return it, it might cost $10. But if the parcel gets all the way to its destination before the problem is identified and we have to return it, it could cost as much as $100. This explains why everything needs to be right first time – any errors in quality that slip through the net make a massive difference and have a huge impact on both cost and customer satisfaction.

Providing great quality is all about focusing on the basics – I can often be heard saying that there's 'nothing basic about the basics'. We need to have the same level of detailed execution on making sure we deliver the basics every day, but we also need to have an eye on how we can continuously tweak and improve the process. When we do both these things, we can all truly say we are having a best day every day – that means being on top of your equipment and IT systems, as well as planning your staff to ensure that the process is flawless every day. And just as every part of our operational process has to work at peak performance, so does our network of people. Our focus on ensuring that our leaders are fit to lead the company helps to create a working experience where our people can operate at their best, promoting physical and mental well-being and encouraging everyone to work together.

The key to consistent quality is routine – it's one of the most powerful tools for removing obstacles, and it helps to make difficult things easy. Without it, we can be overpowered by the pull of non-essential distractions. The physiology of our brain shows that with repetition, the neural synapses are strengthened, and it becomes easier for the brain to activate these connections. That's why world-class athletes, dancers, musicians and business people all practise so much. Mindful routine embeds processes in our brains so we can execute them on autopilot, which frees our brains up to focus on things they can do to make their performance even better. The right routines can enhance productivity by giving us the equivalent of an energy rebate – we're able to seize on new opportunities, because we've already mastered the basics.

Our constant focus on quality is the glue that holds our Big Yellow Machine together. From a process point of view, we ensure that the whole business, all around the world, adopts our global standard operating procedures. It's important to find the fine balance between being local, which means having the best access to customers and people, and also being part of a global network: we need to be centralised and decentralised at the same time. Although we aim for a consistent quality of service around the world, we also enable our leaders to act like owners in their respective countries – we like to set people free so they can apply our global disciplines in the ways that are most appropriate for their cultures.

The quality we deliver affects the reputation of our brand – if you represent DHL Express, you need to be the best in the world. Quality is the cornerstone of excellence for our brand, and our promise reflects this: 'Excellence. Simply Delivered'. If we don't deliver, we suffer the consequences; the way that our people act and the way that we manage the processes, right down to the way that we drive our vehicles all impact on our service quality and the perception of the brand.

Delivering great service quality consistently gets you noticed, but we don't always know how good we are until we are objectively analysed by a credible third party. External awards are the ultimate professional accolade and we regularly shine in them, which is a great motivator for our people. Pat Tan, global head of Customer Service at DHL and inventor of the 'Insanely Customer-centric Culture', began entering us for awards for the quality of our customer service a number of years ago. In 2018 alone, we won over 200 external awards. I'm proud of the fact that we're bold enough to enter external award contests, and I'm even prouder of my teams when they win them!

Ultimately, it's the quality of our service that keeps customers loyal, reduces costs and creates a winning culture. Our key job is to keep our global teams sufficiently motivated that they continue to make delivering great service quality a personal choice, and that requires leaders who don't just *say* that their people are their most important asset – they need to prove it by investing in them. That requires a real love for your business and a genuine care for your people that can't be faked – you have to be prepared to lead by example and get your hands dirty. If you get this right, finding the balance between quality service and cost is simple.

Great service quality is represented by the song 'What the World Needs Now is Love, Sweet Love', a 1965 hit written by Hal David and Burt Bacharach, but that was first recorded and popularised by Jackie DeShannon. I wanted every one of our employees to love our customers, no matter what their role was. Over and over again, I tell people that no matter their actual job, everyone should think of themselves as being in sales. We sing the song to remind us of what we need to give our customers.

WHY FOCUS ON LOYAL CUSTOMERS?

'Excellence. Simply Delivered.' This was the brand promise we introduced in 2010. When our customers saw it, they said, 'Hey, that's you!' I said 'What, the excellence?' they said 'No, the simply!' I've always believed that a simple approach is critical to building customer loyalty – it means that everyone who works for us understands the big picture in broad terms, they know what we are promising to our customers and can also understand the role they need to play in delivering it.

Customer loyalty comes naturally when you have both a world-class service and an awesome people network. In the latter, it's crucial that everyone is well trained and well treated by a leadership that is actively engaged in helping them build their careers and in providing a great experience for our customers. And at DHL, we have that in large measures.

We know that we get it right for our customers on a functional level – our great service quality sees to that! We also spend a disproportionate amount of time focusing on how we can create a real emotional connection with our customers – giving them reasons to believe in and trust the brand and what it stands for. Building that level of brand trust takes focus and hard work, but is the key to winning and keeping customer loyalty. A large part of it is about telling inspiring stories about your brand that accentuate the things you are really good at and that make you stand out from the crowd.

The simplicity of our approach emphasises what Peter Drucker advocated as the one principle of business – to create and keep a customer. We deliver great service quality, we deliver on our promises and we give our customers lots of reasons to love our brand. All this is only possible because of our amazing global teams who all think and act like salespeople, which means focusing on getting to know our customers even better. Because it's simple – if I deliver for them, I will win their loyalty. This philosophy is driven by our leaders, who understand you can only build your business if you let the customers help to shape the brand and give them reasons to stay with you. This is just as true for people who work in functions as it is for the front line – at the end of the day, every one of us is serving the customer.

Loyal customers are represented by the song 'Simplicity' by Bob Seger. His earthy voice and the song's thumping rhythm have moved DHL people into powerful action, everywhere from Singapore to Saskatoon. To this day, I can still feel the adrenaline start to pump when we play the song at our events – I'll never get tired of hearing and singing it.

WHY FOCUS ON A PROFITABLE BUSINESS?

This one is a clear no-brainer. What I've learned about how to make money in business comes down to a few things:

1. Many of us know the old adage that 'Revenue is vanity, but profit is sanity'. Every company wants to grow their revenue, but this can't be the overriding objective – it's crucial that profit is considered. I've seen experienced managers get hooked on the drug of revenue growth, without fully understanding how to convert it into productivity and other cost gains that drive profitable growth. The only real sanity is in earnings before interest and taxes (EBIT).

2. But, as I often joke, you cannot have your cake and EBIT – you have to be constantly watching your cost position. If you want to keep cutting ribbons, you have to keep cutting costs, and the best way to do this is to

make sure that your volume growth is converted into lowering your unit cost. Otherwise, bureaucracy can grow like a weed and create a drag on your organisation in terms of additional costs and non-core productive activity.

3. The truth is that the better you're doing, the easier it is to overlook inefficiencies, but if you do that, everything else will suffer. Financial results are lagging indicators rather than leading indicators, so it's important that a company's leadership is open and straightforward. If the people at the top don't talk straight, then no one in the company will own up to problems, which is how companies start to go downhill. Record profits might mask underlying problems that could actually bring the company down, and financial success can also lead to complacency.

4. For me, pricing is key. As market leaders, you have to set prices that reflect a fair return on capital invested. There has to be a formal process every year to look at a global price increase, which should take into account inflation and exchange rate movements. We have a tender review board to recognise the contribution of our biggest customers, and we treat them accordingly. You need a mechanism that will allow you to account for costs outside your control that you need to pass on. Then it's key to ensure that customers are giving you the volume of business for the prices you have quoted. In a more sophisticated environment, you might even factor in what a customer is willing to pay.

5. Cash flow is reality and a quality indicator because if service is first class, our customers will pay us on time. Cash flow is real money in the bank and cannot be manipulated by accounting conventions – it's a key indicator for analysts

A profitable network is fundamentally about simplicity – Drucker believes that results are the only true sign of excellence, and I tend to agree. That's why I've pushed P&L responsibility down to business units *and* keep a centralised network view – it's a local and global approach. I've made capabilities in pricing and procurement a key priority across the world to ensure that we extract the best possible value from everything we do. When you combine that with a culture that focuses on productivity and service quality, you have a winning formula for profit and growth.

During my career at DHL Express, I've improved profitability in every role I've had. When I became global CEO in 2009, I faced the biggest challenge of my career. We had just lost over €2 billion and were bleeding cash. However, in 2018 we made more than €1.9 billion and generated over €1 billion in free cash flow after investing €1 billion in capital expenditure. Our market share had improved 9 percentage points to 38 per cent and our Active Leadership score among our people had increased 27 percentage points to 87 per cent. How? For me it's simple – motion comes from emotion, so get involved, show your people that you care and the rest will follow.

For the fourth pillar, network profitability, we chose 'Billionaire' by Travie McCoy, featuring Bruno Mars. As with all these songs, I truly believe that the music connects with people at a visceral level. It transcends cultures and boundaries. It makes people want to dance and move. And if people are having fun, it seems clear to me that they will bring a lot more of themselves to their work.

When I delivered my Focus 2010 strategy, I knew that I somehow had to give it a mythological, heroic dimension, so people were truly inspired to become champions in execution. I turned to two of my favourite cinematic icons: Yoda from *Star Wars* and Maximus, from the film *Gladiator*.

In the classic *The Empire Strikes Back*, Yoda provides a memorable instruction to Luke Skywalker before he attempts to raise Luke's X-wing fighter from the swamp where he has crash landed: 'Do. Or do not. There is no try'. Until that point, Yoda has consistently tried to teach Luke to focus on the present and, essentially, to grow up. In this moment, he makes his thoughts clear. The line has become a modern slogan – a reminder that we should totally commit ourselves to what we want to achieve by doing it with all of our concentration and capacity. I would always play the scene at the start of meetings, and also told the leaders that they would succeed if they did all they could with all they had, but that if they had even a tiny bit of doubt, it would destroy them – success would only be certain if they were too. They would usually nod one by one, as they came to understand the power of the instruction.

In the Oscar-winning movie *Gladiator*, Russell Crowe plays a Roman general called Maximus, who has been betrayed by an emperor's corrupt son, who murdered his family. He comes to Rome as a gladiator, in order to seek revenge. In one magnificent and memorable scene, Maximus and a group of fellow gladiators wait in the arena before a fight. As he looks at the gates, Maximus says to his peers, 'You can help me. Whatever comes out of these gates, we've got a better chance of survival if we work together. Do you understand? If we stay together, we survive'. Their opponents then emerge from the gates on multiple chariots, armed with arrows, spears and blades. Maximus consolidates his companions and, with shields raised, urges them to advance towards the chariots with two powerful words, 'As one!'. Needless to say, he and his fellow gladiators win the day.

Those two words sum up both the culture and the fundamental operating principle that would enable us to achieve our ambition: whatever we did, we had to think and act 'as one global network'. To this day, it remains something of a rallying cry, and emphasises the idea that we trust our colleagues to play as one team. For example, when we're moving heavyweight shipments out of the network, some countries will be affected more than others, but that doesn't matter – it's all about the network, and that's how people are incentivised.

I later included more global icons to my messages, in order to add more depth and impact to what I was trying to say. For example, I expressed my belief in every DHL employee in every country around the world by quoting from Lady Gaga who exhorts every person in the audience to reject those who make them feel insignificant and try to remember that each one and every one of them is a superstar.

Every time I play a video clip of this motivational speech by Lady Gaga, I get a cheer from the audience. There's a reason why she has become a global giant: she epitomises the essence of people's dreams and desires, and is able to communicate this spirit in a very uncorporate kind of way.

Another fictional hero I have employed to exemplify our commitment to every single package that is entrusted to us is Arthur Christmas, the title character from the 2011 animated movie. Arthur is the clumsy, fearful, but enthusiastic son of Santa. When, during one of the Christmas delivery operations, a present isn't delivered to a child, Arthur understands his purpose: after all, the only thing that matters is whether the presents are delivered, regardless of how it is done and by whom. Through tenacity and ingenuity, he finds a way to deliver the present to the child on time. Eventually, Arthur happily takes over the entire enterprise as the new Santa. Arthur's mantra is 'I just want it to be perfect for every kid!'. My mantra is, 'I just want it to be perfect for every customer!'. Either way, it seems clear to me that we're both driven by the same spirit of getting it right every time, so that no one is ever disappointed.

As I have said previously, I think everyone should be a salesperson – that's why I also love Leo, the hard-selling business executive who was a featured character in Jim Henson's Muppet Meeting Films, a series of training videos that was commissioned by IBM, before also being licenced to other companies. Leo's enthusiasm, optimism and acceptance of the jargon in his business life impressed us a lot. His best-known appearance was his solo turn in *Sell! Sell! Sell!* in which a low-key speech becomes increasingly frantic. It was this scene that made him a great character that we could use to convey the message that everyone is in sales and that selling and growth is what we should be constantly thinking about.

In meeting after meeting, I told everyone that there was only one strategist at DHL Express, and that was me. I was being humorous, though there was a serious message behind my words – I wanted to make clear that what I really cared about was execution. The message was obvious: everyone is an executor and if they played their role, everything else would take care of itself. It really is that simple.

Sometimes I would surprise myself in those meetings by becoming emotional. My eyes would water and my voice would break as I asked my colleagues, 'Why would anyone want to work anywhere else?' I later learned that these exhibitions of emotion moved the audiences in ways that I could never have anticipated. People had never seen anyone so senior show so much heart and could see my depth of commitment and passion for the mission. I was even more pleased to know that they were also proud to work at DHL and were enormously gratified that their new global CEO shared their feelings. Before I launched Focus 2010, I was thought of as a cold-blooded-do-whatever-it-takes downsizer and turnaround king. After the launch, I became known as the CEO who cared more about DHL Express's success than anyone else in the company, and it made all the difference in the world.

I'm proud to say that nine years later, we're still using the same plan: Focus 2010 has become Focus 2020. We're placing more emphasis on business-to-consumer deliveries as a result of the boom in e-commerce, but the essential principles remain the same. In fact, because global trade is accelerating so rapidly, we're more committed to being number one in international shipping than ever. It's our international domain expertise that accounts for our extraordinary performance, and it's also what will power us forwards in the years ahead.

John Pearson, CEO of DHL Express, Europe and now global CEO, and another 30-year veteran of DHL sums up my leadership impact and style in his own words:

Ken is hands-on but also very much hands-off. When I replaced him in Europe, Ken was still based in Europe. He just stepped back. In fact, when Ken just nods and grunts in response to a question, it means you can go away and do what you believe needs to be done.

As Ken once said to me: 'I'm not here to answer questions. I'm here to ask them'.

Ken's passion for the business is at a similar level to his compassion for people. Ken is at his most vulnerable when he hears of personal setbacks or crises that his people are experiencing.

Ken is famous for his sense of humour and resilience. They enable him to bounce back quickly from any situation. He is as committed to having fun as he is to the bottom-line results. Somehow, Ken has the ability to get people to want to do things that he wants them to do. He gets them to believe it needs to be done and they need to do it. He also gives them the freedom to get it done.

A lot of Ken's impact comes from the simple way he goes about his business. He is not a guy who will put his arm around you or constantly pepper you with affirmation. He talks about big things. He's not into small talk. He maintains a distance but there is an undeniable closeness in one's mutual commitment to each other and the company. When you ask Ken a serious question, you get a serious answer and then the conversation may be over. You have to know when to leave. It's a trait that keeps things sensible and serious.

About three years ago, I approached Ken and suggested that we get a study completed on e-commerce and establish ourselves as a leading player in e-commerce. It was a two-minute discussion. Ken agreed to do it. Six months later we produced a white paper. Then we started riding the slipstream of the e-commerce phenomenon. Since the day he gave the go-ahead, he has made it a core priority. Every week, he asks me about our progress in this regard. We have made incredible progress. We are now acknowledged by the investment community as being strongly poised to exploit the e-commerce wave. Ken's support and advocacy of e-commerce has accelerated our achievements in this regard.

Ken has never been afraid to speak truth to power. If he sees something that needs to be changed, he changes it. Time and time again, I've seen him have the difficult conversations that no one else is prepared to have — even if it wasn't his function. What's more, senior leaders in the company listened to him and took his advice.

One of the best pieces of advice I ever got from Ken was that if you think it's the right thing to do, don't let other people's opinions constrain you. When Ken introduced music and singing to his leadership repertoire, he knew he wasn't great at it. But that wasn't the point. He wanted to demonstrate the importance of having fun and not taking oneself too seriously. It was also a point about courage. He wanted to communicate his self-confidence in a friendly, inviting kind of way. He pulled it off but he didn't know he could pull it off when he started doing it.

KEY LEARNING

- Have a best day every day.
- Find a way to get the message from the CEO to the front line. Songs are good.

- Focusing on quality pays big dividends. Think 1-10-100.
- The key to consistent quality is routine – it's a powerful tool.
- Don't just *say* your people are your most important asset – prove it by investing in them.
- Create a real emotional connection with your customers.
- Revenue is vanity, EBIT is sanity and cash is reality.
- If you want to keep cutting ribbons, you have to keep cutting costs.
- Bureaucracy can grow like a weed, keep busting it.
- The better you're doing, the easier it is to overlook inefficiencies, financials are lagging indicators.

CHAPTER 10:
THE WORLD'S MOST GLOBAL EMPLOYEE ENGAGEMENT PROGRAMME ... EVER

INTRODUCING CIS

> CFO: *'What if we spend all this money on great training for our people and they leave?'*
> CEO: *'What if we don't and they stay?'*
> Ken Allen

I knew we had a powerful strategy in Focus, but a plan on paper is just words until it inspires people into action. And as we focused on being the best international express logistics company in the world, it was crucial that we found a way to engage, excite and inform every single person at DHL to play at that level. But how do you create an engagement experience that is relevant to 100,000 global employees across all functions and at all levels?

The answer was CIS – Certified International Specialist. It's an integrated employee engagement programme that encompasses communication, learning modules, reward and recognition. The vision was simple: to ensure that the Focus strategy is delivered with passion every day by every employee across the globe. It was an internally developed programme that would enable every DHL member to master the fundamentals of international express business, and it would also educate everyone on the heritage and culture of the company. CIS would be layered on top of the Four Pillars and connect them all together. It would be the spark that would ignite our transformation and would help to get us back to the future – back to our customer-obsessed roots, but in a way that worked for our current customers.

Having been with the company for 25 years, I'd worked with the pioneers of DHL's international expansion in the 1970s and 1980s and had participated in the vibrant, 'customer-obsessed', entrepreneurial spirit that had fuelled our global growth. I was convinced that the spirit of DHL's early days was still alive and well in the DHL of 2009, but also believed that we had lost sight of it because we were distracted and were trying to do too much. It was time to return to our roots, but this time we would learn from the past. We would use every technological tool at our disposal, and would get it right first time by tapping into the energy and passion of the 100,000 people we had working for us across the world.

I wanted CIS to educate employees on the various facets of international business and shipping – from how to fill out transportation documents to how international commercial terms worked and the customs clearance processes. More than that, I wanted them to be excited by the great 'Customer-centric Culture' that we had pioneered and become famous for, and for them to feel connected to it. It was also important to me that we ran exactly the same programme in every country – I wanted to duplicate the experience of dealing with DHL and for it to be the same in Toronto, Tokyo or Timbuktu. After all, one ignorant or disengaged employee anywhere in the world could put the whole business at risk.

The mammoth task would require a global army of dedicated specialists who would not falter from the task and would be prepared to go to any length to deliver the Foundation module successfully, on time and on budget. In fact, their roll-out was so successful that the *Guinness Book of Records* deemed their achievement 'unbeatable', which meant that they ruled that it could not be included as a record – which was a record in itself! I'm serious – you just can't make this stuff up! But why, when the vast majority of similar corporate programmes fail miserably, did this one succeed – and continues to do so? And what lessons can other organisations learn from our incredible and successful journey?

DREAM TEAM

To crack this challenge, I would need to assemble a team of creative thinkers who had the vision to see the full potential of CIS as I did, and really give it some legs. I found a mix of internal and external experts – behavioural scientists, strategic change experts, creative designers, film makers, animators and language specialists, all supported by an internal team focusing on international express. They made my idea to turn the entire company into Certified International Specialists, by aligning the love of brand with the power of learning, a reality. As Sue Stoneman of NKD, the learning specialist I brought on board, comments:

> *Ken's belief in the intangible power of motivated people was unwavering. He knew it would work. He brought together a range of talents and instilled in them that same belief. And as the programme took shape, he gave it the total commitment it needed to succeed. If his time was required, he made himself available.*

LEADERSHIP FROM THE TOP

We were aware that 70 per cent of engagement strategies fail as a result of a lack of sponsorship and ownership at the top, so we were determined to make this one different. We worked side by side with the design team all the way through the process, invested time at global board meetings, participated in walk-throughs of activities and content design, and were filmed talking about the business (and refilmed, when messages were changed as part of the development process). We talked passionately about CIS at every possible opportunity and also participated in pilot sessions, took classes, and became accredited to run some of the classes. We became true ambassadors of CIS, and the people in our company noticed – I remain convinced to this day that our passionate belief in the programme was the key to its lasting success. Once the Foundation module was completed, it had to be translated into 42 languages, and some 200 local Country Champions managed local roll-outs to help hit the target of educating 100,000 people in less than a year. The final part of the puzzle was put into place when a team of over 2,000 in-house facilitators, from board members to front-line supervisors, volunteered to deliver the module: the very best of DHL Express talent had stepped up to the plate.

BE CLEAR ABOUT THE END GOAL

Taking 100,000 people offline and putting them through immersive learning is a huge investment, so we had to be certain that the payback would be equally huge. The CIS team began the design work knowing precisely how they would recognise if they had made a wise investment – they chose five strategic measures from their employee opinion survey that they thought indicated employees' understanding and buy-in to the Focus strategy, as well as their passion to deliver it. They also knew the impact that all this would have on Customer Net Promoter scores and the flow-through that there would be to the bottom line. Armed with this information to focus their thinking about the project, the design team ensured that every minute of every hour of learning was specifically targeted at one of the key metrics.

THINK LIKE AN EMPLOYEE

When internal teams start to design orientation programmes, there's always a huge temptation to employ a 'throw in the kitchen sink' mentality, the idea that if you have your employees together for a limited time, you should fill their heads with as much corporate information as possible, until they are close to exploding. However, this is a completely flawed strategy, because the human brain is wired to learn in a particular way – it likes to take in information, process it, filter it and store it, all of which takes time. Most of this processing in the workplace is done subconsciously, perhaps over a coffee break when you're talking to colleagues and not actually thinking about it. The brain also likes messages to be reinforced. Doing things like choosing a few simple messages, building on them over the course of multiple sessions, making links and repeating earlier learning points all add to the brain's ability to retain and recall key information.

People need to understand the story, but they also need to experience what it's like to actually *live* the values and behaviours of the organisation. And if you really want them to internalise new ways of behaving, you should make those new skills and behaviours relevant for them outside work, too. Give people life skills, rather than just skills that will help them in business.

LEAD FROM THE FRONT

Leaders need to be role models for new behaviours. To successfully execute Focus and ensure a high return on the investment in CIS, our leaders needed to embrace a new way of leading. A companion programme to CIS was conceived: the Certified International Manager (CIM) programme ensured that leaders from all levels knew what they needed to do to make CIS successful.

So where to start? I went back to my principles of SELF Reflection to come up with CIS – I believe that this programme, more than anything else, is my enduring legacy to DHL Express. It's been the 'secret sauce' of our turnaround, helping us tap into the intrinsic motivation of our people to do what they love to do and to help them deliver a world-class experience to our customers:

Simplicity – one simple idea: all of our training and the core of our culture will be CIS.

Execution – a unique blend of world-class, immersive training, supported by inspiring internal communications.

Leadership – the only way to roll out such a global culture re-engagement programme is to ensure that every manager, from my Global Management Board to every Country Management Team is helping to actually deliver the programmes.

Focus – it was my personal mission to make everyone a Certified International Specialist and to make this a clear differentiator in the market.

Reflection – this was the question, 'Can we really afford it and will we get the return?' I was reminded of the famous quote: "'What if we give everyone great training and they leave?'"said the CFO. "But what if we don't and they stay?" replied the CEO'.

I also wanted to show my belief in the power of motivated people to transform our fortunes – it's been a long journey, but I've not been disappointed, and nor have Deutsche Post DHL group or our investors.

Here's the short story of CIS: it really is what turned DHL Express around, and I hope you take something from it. It's not for the faint-hearted or those who pretend to be interested in the power of an engaged workforce but aren't really. It's for brave and determined leaders who dream big and want to connect their people to that dream. They are the crazy ones – the ones who are prepared to transform their industries for the better. And I hope this is a story that inspires them to follow their guts and their hearts!

Our ambition was simple: to instil in 100,000 DHL employees, in every corner of the planet, a new sense of pride in becoming a specialist in international express. Everyone would experience the same learning journey, from the long-serving members of the Global Management Board to the newcomer starting on the phones in customer service. At a time when the business was still struggling to achieve profitability, CIS represented an investment of over €100 million. At the time, it was the largest employee engagement programme of its kind in the world. This was a huge sum for what many people regarded as 'just a training programme', but I knew it was much more than this – to me, it was a mass mobilisation of people's hearts and minds. I wanted to demonstrate to our people that their ability to provide world-class customer service was central to our success. And it paid off, big time.

A SOLID FOUNDATION FOR THE FUTURE

If it all starts with motivated people, then what would motivate our global team to turn up every day, deliver more value for their customers and fuel the long-term success of DHL Express? The CIS project established three guiding principles:

1. Focus on a few, simple, relevant messages to inspire employees to take positive action.
2. Encompass heart and brain: friendly learning and engagement techniques that would significantly enhance buy-in, recall and retention of the key messages.
3. Include immersive, experiential learning and communications approaches to encourage employees to make personal changes and inspire actions to improve service to customers.

These principles guided the design of our first stage, CIS Foundation, during which we asked ourselves the following compelling questions:

*   What is our brand heritage?
*   What do we want to be famous for? How well are we delivering this to our customers?
*   What do we need to know to be International Specialists?

With the 'what' of the module firmly in place, our attention turned to the 'how':

*   How do we need to behave to be International Specialists? What more can we do to show our customers we are 'Insanely Customer-centric'?
*   How can we display speed, passion, can-do and right first time in our role, every day?

Creating the learning journey and narrative for the Foundation was the more straightforward part of the challenge; designing globally relevant and sensitive engagement and learning experiences was much more challenging. The team thought of ways to appeal to all DHL employees, regardless of culture or geography, incorporating many different means of engaging their attention, stimuli from film to animation, board games to reflection time – all of which were aimed at deepening and fast-tracking the individual's learning experience. Focusing on what every individual could do to positively impact the DHL Express customer experience, the learning became 'real' for all employees, and also helped them to see how they could get involved through the use of real-life examples.

A PASSPORT TO SUCCESS

Another part of the execution was to ensure the learning was taken seriously. Many of our 100,000-strong team have a similarly limited academic history to me, but I wanted my people who become 'Certified' to feel like they had really achieved something and had 'graduated with honours' – so assessments were incorporated at the end of the module to recognise and value their achievement. Again, I needed a creative device to represent this. The now iconic red Passport to Success was issued, in which participants would collect stamps of achievement as they passed through the full curriculum of modules. It did that, but it also went way further – it gives a sense of belonging and family to employees around the world. Even today, over ten years after the programme was first introduced, you can ask any DHL person you meet, anywhere in the world to produce their CIS passport and they'll do it with pride. Every course has a visa that is stuck in the passport, starting with the Foundation and Welcome modules through to facilitated training, Certified International Manager and all other CIS programmes and engagement initiatives. On many occasions, managers and supervisors are asked to sign congratulatory notes in the passport – and they are very happy to do so.

BY EXPRESS PEOPLE FOR EXPRESS PEOPLE

I knew that the key to engaging with our workforce at a local level was to have CIS delivered 'by Express people to Express people' to ensure an authentic delivery – that was my main execution strategy. To make this a reality, some 2,000 global facilitators were trained and accredited to run the Foundation module – this would launch CIS into the DHL firmament. And to lead from the top, I mandated that leaders get involved at all stages, appearing in the videos of the events that are sent to the network around the world. The result was that everyone knew my leadership team was approachable and 100 per cent on board with the programme – it was a major step that helped promote the kind of open, accessible culture I wanted. Now, wherever we are in the world our teams recognise us and have no worry about stopping us to ask if they can take a selfie with us or if we could say a few words that they could share with their teams on their return home. There is an affectionate familiarity between global leadership and the front line because people feel like they know us, and that's how I want it to stay – like one big, connected family.

GETTING CREATIVE

Creativity has been a vital part of our execution of CIS. I wanted to design some iconic creative devices that would link all the modules together and needed a vehicle that would resonate with my teams around the globe and remind them of the DHL Express Unique Value. So along with creative partners Maverick, we brought the DHL Express Superhero characters to life to provide role models of what Certified International Specialists look and feel like. Maverick's CEO Owen Rees explains:

Ken was asking his people to be everyday heroes to the people around them. That's what these characters represent. He wanted people to believe in their own super powers; to be role models for each other so everyone aspires to be great. Ken supported the development of something really special when he asked us to bring this idea to life. Getting the characters right was as important as creating a new Pixar family.

These characters have become part of the DHL Express folklore through animated films, adding excitement, humour and intrigue to the programme. Equally important was telling key parts of the story through professional-quality investigative journalist-style films.

MAKING IT MODULAR

The next challenge for CIS was to build a bespoke Welcome to My Country module for all 220 countries. This required a standardised format that could also house local country facts and figures – a section that covered the history of DHL in that area, introducing key local customer organisations and sectors, explaining the local organisational structure, outlining local initiatives and exploring key performance measures. The aim was to quickly engage employees with their local challenges and opportunities, but always focusing on the core message, 'What can you do to make things better for our customers?'.

Another challenge was to create functional training curriculums for all employees, from sales to finance and operations to HR. A series of CIS modules ensured that all our employees had the right skills, knowledge and behaviours to say they were Certified International Specialists in their field of expertise. And of course, all modules contain an assessment that would give them another stamp in the Passport to Success.

CIM SUPERVISORY ACADEMY – HARDWIRING A CULTURAL PHENOMENON

During my career, one of my biggest realisations was that if I talk to a front-line person, they'll listen. But if their supervisor shares the same messages about how great the company is, that takes the organisation to a whole new level. Nothing motivates someone more than their immediate supervisor. That's the real reason why people join or leave a company.

I hope one of my lasting legacies will be the game-changing Supervisory Excellence programme I pioneered for our front-line supervisors. They are the ladies and gentlemen who, day in and day out, keep my great team working, motivated and doing whatever it takes for our customers. If you do nothing else as a result of reading *Radical Simplicity*, spend a week out there working shoulder to shoulder with your supervisors. See what they do, the challenges they face and the massive impact they have on motivation. Then make yourself a commitment to give them all the tools, skills, knowledge and belief they need to drive your business forward. It will be the best week of your life and the best decision you will ever make.

By 2014 our employee engagement scores were making a seismic shift in the right direction; we'd done a great job at engaging our people and enhancing their natural talents. I needed this revitalised, 'Insanely Customer-centric Culture' to stick; it had to outlast me and my senior leadership team. We lit the blue touch paper and now it had to burn bright across the organisation every single day. CIS had started us on the journey to becoming the employee- and customer-centric culture that we wanted to be. But we found that, although we had involved the whole network, some people were still more engaged and involved than others.

To change this, we would need to introduce an extra step that would integrate a 'top down' learning culture; engaging those at management level who in turn would influence front-line workers. Our Employee Opinion Scores suggested that, at any one time, 21 per cent of employees globally were 'not engaged' at work. This told me I was still sitting on an immense, untapped reservoir of potential performance – which, if I believe the management literature, could translate to as much as 40 per cent higher productivity in operational roles, 49 per cent more profit in general management roles and 67 per cent more revenue in sales roles.

I thought long and hard and worked with Sue and her team at NKD to try and understand what we needed to do to reinforce this CIS culture. We kept coming back to one simple conclusion. The lynchpin to tapping into this potential upturn in performance lay in the hands of our 15,000–20,000 people employed in 'supervisory' level roles – team leaders, supervisors and some operational managers. We realised that it's these critical roles that build trust at the front line, they inspire performance and drive improved productivity. These individuals are the 'power house' of our organisation; how they behave with their teams today significantly impacts our bottom line tomorrow.

Like many other organisations, we realised we had significantly underinvested in this key community of front-line leaders. There was an urgent need to 'professionalise' our approach to 'supervising' our front-line teams. This applied equally to the existing population and to our newly appointed supervisors. They needed to gain or refresh core team management skills, understand the key processes required to manage well and gather the practical tools that would enable them to drive the highest levels of performance at their local levels.

This population were already due to attend our CIM orientation programme which sets the scene for what living our guiding leadership philosophy of Respect and Results means in their roles. But we needed more than that – so we set about designing a transformational, modular and self-directed learning experience to reconnect them with the core deliverables of their role:

1. Managing and inspiring their teams.
2. Managing quality at a local level.
3. Creating 'Insanely Customer-centric Culture' at a local level.
4. Driving high performance through their teams.
5. Delivering their people, customer, operational and financial key performance indicators.
6. Managing corporate responsibility – representing the World at its Best.

The aim of the programme was two-fold:

For new supervisors and team leaders, we wanted to provide them with the best support as they made the career-defining transition into the roles. We wanted to provide them with the skills and knowledge to engage their teams and drive high performance – getting them confident and productive in their new roles as quickly as possible.

And for our existing supervisors and team leaders, we wanted to refresh and enhance their existing leadership skills and knowledge, and refocus them on the core deliverables of their roles. We needed to develop a challenging, extremely practical, rewarding and high-impact programme. Key was getting the balance of inspiring them and giving them practical tools they could quickly apply after their modules.

So we went back to basics and set ourselves the aim of building the best-ever supervisory development programme – a holistic 'Leadership 101 Programme' designed especially for them. More than that, we recognised that many of our front-line supervisors had left school at a young age so it was important to them to get some external recognition and validation of their newly honed skills. So we worked with country accreditation professionals to make sure we could get everything they learned and applied accredited, making up a qualification equivalent to two-thirds of a university degree. We also set ourselves the challenge of creating something that was a distinctive and memorable experience for this audience, different to CIM – this programme would become the seminal programme of a DHL Express manager's career.

We built the programme around the Four Pillars of Focus:

1) Personal Excellence – It's All About YOU!
2) People Excellence – It's All About Our People.
3) Service Excellence – It's All About Our Service Quality.
4) Operational Excellence – It's All About Delivery.

And we blended the delivery approach to provide key inputs and ideas, and practise new skills and attitudes. Some are face-to-face modules, some e-learning, some self-directed learning through personal e-tablets; each delivered at a time when supervisors most need it and can apply it in their roles. The programme is supported by manager and peer coaching, work-based assignments and Learning Networks to ensure the skills are retained and used by participants.

The success of the programme was dependent on participants' one-to-one coaching sessions with their sponsoring managers who would provide vital ongoing developmental support, and encourage the desired behaviours and skills to materialise. What we quickly realised was that many of the supervisors' managers lacked the coaching skills needed, so we developed our three-day 'Coaching for Success' module that all sponsoring managers had to complete prior to their supervisor starting the programme. Not only was this great for the supervisors, it also had a positive effect on the overall engagement of our front-line teams as their managers started to adopt a coaching approach in everything they did. A great return on investment for us!

We also wanted to be able to measure how effectively the new skills and tools were being applied back at work, so we built a series of 'Back at Work Challenges' – work-based assignments to ensure the learning was applied, which were measured by the sponsoring manager and signed off on their successful demonstration of competency. This 'sign off' became a key part of the ongoing coaching sessions. And to keep the supervisors connected and supported, we put in place a Learning Network. This made use of Skype and other conferencing technology to develop team-based learning – discussing how to transfer learning to specific work-based challenges and maintain motivation levels. And it worked.

We involved our supervisory control group – 60 supervisors representing all functions and geographies – to help co-create the entire 12-month programme; taking their input, building solutions, piloting them with this group, and then refining the programme based on their feedback. The result is a programme that is essentially built for them, by them – stretching their thinking, honing their skills, and most importantly, building a strong People Network across this critical population of front-line leaders.

So far we have seen some 750 people graduate from the programme – and when I say graduate, I mean it. We do the whole thing, caps and gowns, valedictorian speeches, and of course, a recognised qualification. We make a real party of it, to celebrate the blood, sweat and tears they have put into the programme. We show them how much we value them and the support they give to our front-line teams. We make sure they know they are the guardians of our CIS culture, they make it real every day for each and every employee and they hold our future success in their hands. We applaud and honour them for that.

THE CIS FUTURE

When it comes to execution, we never stand still, and I regularly challenge the team to add the latest approaches and technology that will help to keep the CIS programme fresh and relevant. We've continued to pioneer, bringing on board new specialist partners to our core team to meet the evolving needs of our audience. So just as DHL Express is a customer-focused business, my CIS team is audience-focused in everything that they do. An exciting new digital future for CIS is emerging, which involves new media, virtual reality experiences, online opportunities to share and connect and other ways to contribute to building the CIS culture. Relevant, innovative and exciting execution is at the heart of our CIS approach, but however the message is delivered, the power of motivated people will always be the core reason why we're doing it – the fact that it's a world-changing philosophy that fuels our success at DHL Express.

People often ask me why CIS turned into such an amazing success, and I tell them that it worked because it was such a simple strategy – a brilliantly designed and executed programme, and a CEO's dream. It delivered enviable results, and continues to do so to this day. So why then, when the vast majority of other similar corporate programmes fail miserably, did this one succeed and continue to succeed? And what lessons can other organisations learn from our incredible and successful journey?

We all know that this kind of success doesn't happen without leadership and commitment, yet it's easy to say and simple to understand, but somehow really difficult to deliver. I encouraged my managers to embrace the journey and, more importantly, to stick with it. Any programme of this size and scale will hit some bumps and detours, but the skill is to recognise them when they come along before deciding if they detract from or enhance the programme and then adapt it accordingly. And that's what we did – we stuck with it.

As a result, we had some great and unexpected outcomes. Our Foundation module naturally evolved into an onboarding programme for new recruits, once a few minor alterations had been made to accommodate their lack of knowledge. And the CIS Facilitation was a great accelerator of management learning – after all, the best way to learn is to teach others, and it became a springboard for talent management. Additionally, providing leaders with both an approach and core coaching skills is an established way to embed new behaviours.

Why has all this been so effective? It's simple – it's because my global management team has been irrevocably committed to it. They know that the modelling of the new culture and behaviours will always be central to DHL's ongoing transformation, and it's now just the way we do things around here. A huge part of the success of the programme was about ensuring that everyday conversations in our company used the language of CIS as part of the vernacular.

YOU NEED TO TALK THE TALK IF YOU WANT PEOPLE TO WALK THE WALK

A key part of leadership is being able to evolve one's language in a way that empowers people to win. Champion teams and champion companies have their own vocabulary. The language that you use defines the world in which you live. At DHL, CIS cuts across 47 languages. Anywhere you go in the world, you'll hear the same phrases, no matter what the national vernacular:

- 'Insanely customer-centric'.
- Superstars of international express delivery.
- Right first time.
- Have a great day every day.
- Everyone is a salesperson.
- Results are the only true sign of excellence.
- Our three bottom lines are provider of choice, employer of choice, investment of choice.
- KPH – knowledgeable, polite and helpful.
- Great service quality.
- The Big Yellow Machine – profit through process.
- Think global. Act local. Stay close to the customer.
- We have a strategic plan. It's called doing things.
- You cannot shrink to greatness.
- Good is the enemy of great.
- Sell, sell, sell.
- If you want to keep cutting ribbons, you have to keep cutting costs.
- The purpose of a business is to create and keep a customer.
- Customer is king.

I believe that CIS has been a revolution in the way multinational companies can engage with their people all over the world. As usual, Charlie Dobbie puts it best:

I recall that Ken, John Pearson and myself were sitting around a boardroom table in Bonn. We were looking for a way to energise and motivate our people through this challenging time. That's when we thought about CIS (Certified International Specialist), a training programme that had been organised in the US to educate people on our international business. It became the most brilliant enabler and unifier of people that I've ever seen. It resonated with people because it came from our collective experience. It rang true. It was tailored for every one of us. It can't be imitated because it's driven by our people. They love it and they live it.

I remember Ken saying that CIS was about taking the best attributes of our past and bringing them with us into the future. That's exactly what it's done.

After nine years, I can tell you without doubt that CIS is the most incredible thing I've ever had the privilege to work on. It has had a huge impact on helping the customer-centric, international mindset to be hardwired into the organisation. We are not yet where we want to be, but we're definitely a long way from where we were. Every time I thought we had cracked the code, I saw new opportunities and challenged the team to think even more innovatively or to increase the scope of the project even further. And most staggeringly, we went from nothing to a programme that was launched in 200 countries and translated into 42 different languages in less than a year. It was at that point that I realised I needed my most senior leaders to deliver the first modules – which meant that I had to skill up 700 leaders in one go. The ability of my team to respond and manage the design and logistics of executing a programme this complex has been jaw-droppingly inspiring. If I'm honest, it's this degree of commitment from my internal team and my external trusted partners that has made all the difference to our CIS journey.

I'm a man who lives by the acronym KYN, which stands for 'Know Your Numbers'. I live or die by the tangibles and measurables of our equipment and technologies, and by performance scorecards. However, I believe even more strongly in the power of motivated people, and their commitment to CIS and the execution of our promise to our customers have made all the difference. Another great thing about CIS is the way it has completely changed how I'm regarded by many people at DHL – it has brought me into the hearts and minds. I personally appear in much of the video material and have made it my job to try to convey a serious message in an entertaining of way. I'm especially delighted when I show up to events and people expect me to start singing the songs that symbolise our Four Pillars!

Ten years on from the establishment of CIS, DHL was voted the sixth best place to work in the world by *Fortune* magazine. Just imagine that – a global business that is all about how to shift boxes from one place to another, work that is often monotonous, usually laborious and always tiring – voted the sixth best place to work, anywhere in the world! I hope that, one day, in the textbooks, under 'the right way to do a global company transformation' you will find DHL Express writ large – not just for me, but in recognition of the tens of thousands of people who pulled together to help pull it off! Without introducing new products, without opening new offices, without breakthrough technology, without slashing prices and without punishing cost management programmes, my team and my people have completely transformed our business in ten years, turning a €500 million loss into an impressive €1.95 billion EBIT. This amazing group of like-minded people needs to be recognised for their incredible achievement.

CEOs often say their people are their strongest competitive advantage, but I don't just say it – I categorically *know* it. The CIS programme has been the fuel that has energised the power of my 'Insanely Customer-centric' 100,000-strong global team, so they all know to play their part in creating this phenomenal turnaround story. They are my inspiration and it's the greatest privilege to have worked alongside them and been part of possibly the most successful company turnaround in the last 30 years!

And the legacy of CIS continues to build. In normal corporate life, if something is successful in one division, it's a sure-fire reason NOT to adopt it in another. But that's not been the case with CIS at Deutsche Post DHL (DPDHL) Group.

Frank Appel, global CEO of DPDHL Group, recognised the year-on-year success CIS was having in DHL Express across our key measures – our three bottom lines of Employer, Provider and Investment of Choice. He made the decision to expand the concept across all group divisions. So confident was he in the concept that he name-checked CIS as the key thrust of the 'Connect' element of his strategy 2020, Focus:Connect:Grow, when he unveiled it to analysts and the business press.

Since then, each of the family of divisions that make up DPDHL Group has launched their own Certified programme with the aim of achieving the same results as DHL Express. And Frank's guiding hand is now firmly on the CIS tiller, shaping the DPDHL Group culture by chairing a quarterly group-wide Certified Board Meeting.

Like any family, our Express CIS team has collaborated with each division to help them create a Certified framework that works for them – embracing their own values and strategies. The result is a connected, group-wide CIS culture. All divisions now have their own version of the CIS Foundation module and have adopted our CIM Leadership approach to embed our leadership philosophy of Respect and Results. As divisions sponsor and build new programmes, the Certified Board collaborate, share and steal content with pride, making sure we all benefit from all new developments and innovations. And for the corporate functions, cross-divisional modules support our HR, Finance and IT functions.

All of this activity is designed to provide our combined 550,000 employees with a common induction experience and to be led by a team of leaders who actively demonstrate our Respect and Results leadership behaviours. And to date, these programmes have been delivering for other divisions the same level of performance and engagement uplift we saw across Express in our first three years.

All going to prove you can't keep a good idea down!

KEY LEARNING

- Engage, excite and inspire every single person in your organisation.
- 70 per cent of engagement strategies fail as a result of a lack of sponsorship and ownership at the top. Lead from the front.
- Know precisely how you will measure success of your engagement.
- Focus on a few simple relevant messages to inspire employees to take positive action.
- Encompass heart and brain.
- Include immersive, experiential learning and communications approaches.
- Enable people to graduate with honours – recognition.
- Encourage managers to embrace the journey and, more importantly, to stick with it.

CHAPTER 11:
BECOMING WORLD CLASS
GOOD IS THE ENEMY OF GREAT

There is no greatness where there is not
Simplicity, Goodness and Truth.
　　Leo Tolstoy

In 2018 we became the most profitable express company in the world – as Pete Drucker says, 'results are the only true sign of excellence' – but those results are the final product of an organisation that is firing in all cylinders and striving to be world class in every function.

It does not come overnight, but that is why it is so powerful and protecting. It comes from an excited and motivated organisation that looks at its colleagues and sees them improving and wants to do the same – no jealousy, just positive competition to be the best.

And it all comes from within. One of my favourite examples is Debbie Goward who runs our global financial business. She is a total customer advocate: if one shipment has a problem she is on it and if it's not fixed, she is on to me! All in a very positive way which really helps me improve service and strive never to lose a customer – ever. Debbie's team have a fantastic retention rate and relationships with its customers.

Then there is Pat Tan, global head of Customer Service (she also runs Customer Service in Asia to keep close to the business). As I mentioned earlier, she was the architect of our 'Insanely Customer-centric Culture' – 'I triple C' as everyone calls it. She is the epitome of continuous improvement; she built our processes and systems based on visiting best-in-class operations. Then she implemented them globally and over time they became world class to the extent that those companies come to visit us.

Next she encouraged all our operations around the world to apply for external awards to verify the effectiveness of our customer services versus best-in-class in every industry, not just the express competitors. In 2018 we won over 200 awards globally. This encouraged our HR community to do the same thing. Under the leadership of Regine Buettner, our global Head of HR, we had already introduced world-class training and processes under the CIS banner and a number of countries were already 'Best Place to Work' or 'Top Employer'. So she instigated a global push and in 2018 we won 160 awards globally.

It is not the awards per se, it is the massive surge in employee engagement and pride when they apply for the awards – you can feel the excitement building and the desire to have their function recognised as best-in-class. This is also an external validation that our approach and processes are the best rather than just internal key performance indicators.

So this approach permeates the entire organisation. Another area where I believe we are world class is pricing. It's a critical but often subsumed discipline hidden away in finance or commercial, but one that really deserves to be a distinct discipline on its own as it has to be incredibly close to the market and our customers, It also needs to be financially disciplined to understand true cost drivers and not accounting conventions, as well as work with operations to understand our competitive advantages and what customers are prepared to pay for.

Mark James and his team have elevated pricing at DHL to be a key differentiator and business partner, building a global pricing matrix that has to take into account exchange rate fluctuations, fuel price movements, delivery complexity and cost differentials by country and location within the country (major business centres versus remote rural locations) and line-haul routings, etc. It is incredibly complicated. But that is just the start: then you have to manage tenders and competitor moves, willingness to pay (the value of your service to their business), promotions and other business stimulations.

When people look at a company they think about its core business – logistics or manufacturing or e-commerce and so on. But within a business of our size and complexity, we have so many opportunities to build world-class functions for any discipline. We are managing one of the best-known international brands on the planet with a value of over €15 billion. We have to manage sponsorship relationships with major entities such as Manchester United football team, Formula E and Formula 1, but we also have to provide guidelines and flexibility for local opportunities. This is the essence of thinking global, acting local.

Then there is tax – yes I know, 'boring' – but we have operations in every country in the world plus hubs and aviation and line-haul networks that all have to be integrated and allocated and then agreed with the tax authorities. We have transfer pricing arrangements with just about every country in the world and all that needs to be centrally controlled and locally managed, AND we are part of a bigger group that has to manage overall tax strategy. Fascinating if tax is what turns you on.

We also need to consider finance. In some years our EBIT is impacted by hundreds of millions just by exchange rate fluctuations. We have to comply with global and local accounting conventions in every country on the planet. We may pick up in America and bill in Australia. There are multiple shared service centres around the globe to maximise efficiency and constantly improve processes.

We have to manage 2.6 million customers in almost every currency and collect it all within 30 days. We have to fund and justify €1 billion in capital expenditure every year and occasionally take the opportunity to buy 14 Boeing 777 aircraft if it makes financial sense and we can convince global treasury. Then we have to explain it to the analysts as well. There is nothing boring about accounting in DHL.

Talking about aviation, we spend over €4 billion a year on our 'virtual airline', which we believe is a unique differentiator in our industry. This has been built up by a team of experts under Charlie Dobbie, and includes Neil Ferguson and Geoff Kehr. We are one of the top three international cargo carriers in the world and are associated with 17 airlines registered in 11 countries. We also generate over €1 billion in revenue by selling any spare capacity on our flights to forwarders and ad hoc customers. John Roach and his Air Cargo Sales (ACS) team are an excellent example of entrepreneurship in our business.

We constantly have to be on top of quality: monitoring every shipment and providing actionable feedback to ensure we proactively fix or notify our customers is a crucial element and a global undertaking. We rely on our country and regional teams to execute, supplemented by our Global Quality Control Centres that monitor 24/7 and are always looking for the latest technology to incrementally improve.

Which brings me to IT. Protecting the netwoek from any type of security threat when we are operating in virtually every country in the world is a key element of our strategy. We work with various governments to monitor cyber threats and strive to improve the latest software to give maximum resilience – a never-ending task for our team of talented IT professionals. We have also developed EGAP – the Express Global Application Platform. It has taken ten years but now we have a high degree of standardised systems making it easier to roll out upgrades and increase our cost effectiveness.

I think our operations and sales organisations have generally been world class from the start. The operation was built organically and relied on the culture of the company to connect the world and build out to a new global offering. From a sales perspective our people have always been incredibly close to our customers and they ensure that we are always at the forefront of new opportunities such as the e-commerce boom we are currently witnessing.

THE FOUR BOTTOM LINES

At DHL we have four bottom lines keeping us on track, which act as our 'checklist of winning':

1. **The financial bottom line**. Is our revenue and profitability growing?
2. **The customer bottom line**. Is their satisfaction growing? The biggest single reflection of this is market share – if I'm simultaneously growing profitability and market share, I'm earning customer satisfaction because of my superior service offering rather then buying it.
3. **The employer bottom line**. Are we employer of choice? Do we have low levels of staff turnover? Do we win external awards? Are we sustaining high engagement scores with our people, and do they enjoy working for us?
4. **The social bottom line.** What are we doing for civilisation more generally? Are our employees interested in giving back to their communities and are we making the world a better place? This is harder to measure, because it's as much a feeling as a fact, but it's still up to us to encourage it.

FOCUS ON DOING THE RIGHT THINGS RIGHT

We're in the business of making big bets – every year, we make decisions on where to spend billions of euros. It's inevitable that we'll make mistakes, but mistakes are not always failures, because they provide opportunities to do something better the next time. Over the past ten years at DHL, we've had to clean up a lot of mistakes that were made in the first decade of this century.

If you don't keep investing, you won't keep growing – you can only grow as fast as your ability to bring on the right talent and build the right infrastructure. Confidence in your vision is the antidote to failure – it's ambivalence and dithering in the face of opportunity that will kill you. Growth companies believe in their model and have the results to prove it, but there's always a lag at the beginning of a cycle as effort and investment precede outcomes – and that's when your faith needs to be at its highest.

We're always trying to give our customers the best service. Our strength is that we're an industry leader, and we've codified our strategy in a plan that we roll out to every leader, every year. We measure everything. Obviously, things will go wrong sometimes, but I never worry that we've got it all wrong, because we're too diligent for that. I also don't worry that someone will disrupt our business. Part of the reason I think this is the case is that a lot of the new technologies don't actually displace anybody; for example, Facebook may have accelerated the decline of traditional media, but it has also brought billions of people closer together.

Revolutions may put some people out of business, but more often they create opportunities. Whether it's the ecosystem provided by the Apple App Store, Google maps or the high-performance electric vehicles developed by Tesla, each of these innovations has created exponentially more opportunities than it has destroyed.

So I believe that there is no point in worrying about the speed of change, and that if we instead focus on doing the right things right, we'll always be at the forefront of change. Let other people worry about your speed of change; the truth is that new technology benefits those companies that are already further ahead, because they are the ones that have the resources and the capability to embrace change.

QUALITY IS A LEADING INDICATOR, FINANCIAL RESULTS ARE A LAGGING INDICATOR

The first thing I did when I became CEO that no one else does was to lay down my financial goals for the next five years, in granular detail. To other people, this may have seemed outlandishly ambitious, but to me, it was plain obvious. As Alan Kay said, 'the best way to predict the future is to invent it'.

As people become more successful, they do more of what they *want* to do for the company, but not what they *need* to do. My job is to keep everyone focused on what's best for DHL, because we cannot take our eye off our mission of being the best international express company in the world. In every conversation with every DHL worker, I ask the same question over and over again: 'How can we make things better — for ourselves, for our customers and for the world?'

Over the past ten years, I've focused on just two or three things each year. Some people talk about focus, but then they formulate 20 priorities, with ten sub-priorities for each priority. Their personal preferences might also interfere with the organisation's goals – I want people to do what's right for the organisation as a whole. For example, if I have a problem at our hub in Leipzig, Germany, I'll want people to focus their effort on that, rather than on where they would like to focus their efforts. We need to fix *what* needs fixing *when* it needs fixing.

While our theme every year is 'focus', we also have a sub-theme each year. For example, in 2018 we pivoted from 'brand boost' to 'quality boost'. In 2017, we picked up a huge amount of business from TNT Express because of the challenges they were experiencing, we had three major hubs that came online at the same time, and there was a surge in the e-commerce business. Believe it or not, the business in 'fidget spinners', the small toy that became a global craze, placed a strain on our global facilities – we were moving literally tons of them.

The move towards global e-commerce is making the peaks in our business even more accentuated. The location and availability of the customer is changing dramatically, and mobile technology is also changing the game. At DHL, we plan to increasingly use the power of digitisation and big data as a way to achieve 'proactive quality' and to alert our people to problems before they occur. For example, if we pick up a package in London that's going to Canada, does it have an exit scan from Heathrow and an arrival scan in Canada? If not, it will generate a trace and notify the stations, as well as logging a report on the system. We expect this part of our business to make a big difference to our quality in the future.

I fully expect that what e-commerce will do to the demand side of our business, big data and predictive analytics will do to the supply side. Together they add up to a fantastic future for DHL Express. Algorithms are going to do what people are currently doing – the quality will be built into the process and the system.

As I've said before, there is a great power in laying out your goals and financial plans clearly so that everyone can see where we stand – and where we're going. Our latest Focus brochure continues to look to the future, with deliverables right through to 2020.

		EBIT Target €	EBIT Achieved €
2015	Renewal	1.5 billion	1.4 billion
2016	Yield Boost	1.5 billion	1.6 billion
2017	Volume Boost	1.6 billion	1.7 billion
2018	Quality Boost	1.7 billion	1.9 billion
2019	Supervisory	1.9 billion	?
2020	Reflection	2.0 billion	?

THERE IS NO TRUER PHRASE IN BUSINESS THAN 'GOOD IS THE ENEMY OF GREAT'

I don't think that a lot of people truly want to be great – or they may want to be, but not enough to pay the price for it. Great results require great effort. Every year at DHL, we bring our top salespeople together to celebrate their achievements as part of our Sales Champions Club – the people who attend the meeting will tell you how important it is to the organisation. In May 2018, the celebration took place in Athens in Greece, and four of our eight global board members were present. I asked the audience, 'How many of you love to win?' Obviously, all the hands went up. Then I asked, 'How many of you love to train hard?' Again, all the hands went up – it was an indication that they understood that talent is merely a starting point. Every day, DHL employees demonstrate that attitude and effort are everything, and that adversity is nothing but an invitation to show how remarkable they can be. As I listened to their stories that day, I felt an incredible kinship with them. When you have great talent working for you, your mandate must always be to develop it further. You have to expand your people's capacity by expanding the scope of their role.

I like to say that DHL is the best in the world but it's also the world at its best. If you've got highly motivated people, they'll take care of everything else, because their natural curiosity will drive them to find the best way forward. In a company like DHL, that has achieved such a marvellous turnaround, there are many people who think we should just consolidate our gains and cruise, but each day I look at my role as if it's my first day as CEO and ask myself what I can do to improve the business. If there's something we could be doing better, I want to find it before the competition does; no matter how good we are, we can always be better.

THE POWER OF MUSIC

When our people hear the songs that epitomise each of the Four Pillars, they immediately think of what they mean – it's a shortcut to their emotions and their eagerness to act. It humanises the message and is unforgettable. It's remarkable how the songs motivate front-line people all over the world, from Cape Town to Copenhagen. Even now, every time I hear them, I want to do something extraordinary – and I know that 100,000 other people do too. It's inspirational karaoke on a massive scale.

I can barely carry a tune, but despite that, I'm now known as 'the singing CEO' because I'm continually singing the songs that epitomise our pillars. I remember the first time I sang 'Ain't No Mountain High Enough' to the Country Managers and senior members of the company in July 2010. It was in London at the opening evening of a three-day offsite. I dressed up like Frank Sinatra and sang with a piano accompaniment, played by Faruk Akosman, my senior communication resource person. The audience was entertained and stunned, but I had also made my point effectively: do whatever it takes to get the message out there. The moral of the story is that we shouldn't let our self-consciousness get in the way of connecting with people.

ALL YOU NEED IS LOVE

The people who do the hardest work deserve the most credit. I'm determined to give it to them because I know it will be reciprocated. I see it and feel it at every DHL event. Total engagement is a powerful competitive advantage, which is why motivated people is my number one priority. One thing that helps to keep us on track is our annual employee engagement survey. We're always chasing an approval rating of over 80 per cent, and asking the same questions every year, and being diligent about analysing the results keeps us focused. We scrutinise each country, and within each country we scrutinise each function – we're always trying to get incrementally better.

No matter what business you're in, you should be on the hunt for the best talent. This means that in a way, DHL is in competition with companies in many different areas of business, because we're targeting the same talent in sales, IT, finance and operations. That's why I'm so committed to being visible in the marketplace and am such a strong supporter of external awards – every news story is an opportunity to increase our reputation among the most talented people in business.

Our efforts are paying off: in 2018 DHL was voted by the Great Place To Work Institute as the sixth best place in the world to work. In Latin America, we were number seven. And in Asia, we were number two, behind Hilton Hotels. I won't be satisfied until we're number one everywhere – if we become known as one of the best places to work in the world, we'll attract the best talent in the world. And if we attract the best talent in the world, the customers, the market share, the revenue and the quality will follow. It takes a long time to get these messages into the organisation and down to the front line, so we have to be relentless in communicating and reinforcing them.

In every staff meeting, I ask people to look at themselves and answer a few questions: are they like Yoda, executing with boldness and self-belief? Is everyone being an Arthur? Do they all feel sick to their stomach if we lose a shipment or fail a customer? And what does being 'Insanely Customer-centric' really mean to them and how are they committing to it? We want everyone to be so happy about working for DHL that they ensure our company is the world at its best. Happy people make customers happy, and they do this by delivering what the customers are paying for.

Competing with UPS and FedEx is a huge challenge, but we're up to it. They are iconic examples of excellence themselves – UPS is the most efficient service company in the world and FedEx is a powerful sales and marketing machine – but the best way for us to stay ahead of them is to keep on focusing on being 'Insanely Customer-centric' and on listening to what our front-line people are telling us about what our customers need.

I'm asking our people to be everyday heroes – that's the imagery that I use in our training courses and all my other communications. I want them to believe in their own superpowers and to be role models for each other, so that everyone aspires to be great. I've said that it's a virtuous cycle: my idea is that if we raise the performance of every person in the organisation, they will all want to create something special.

A core part of my agenda is that I want people to commit to a cause that's worthy of their life – I want them to feel like they're making a real difference. 'Connecting People, Improving Lives' is not just an advertising slogan – it's what we think about every single day. The challenge is to keep this vision at the front of our minds, whether we're battling the traffic in London or navigating the monsoons in India.

KEY LEARNING

- Mistakes are not failures: they're opportunities to do something better the next time.
- Focus on doing the right things in the right way and you'll be at forefront of change.
- The more you achieve, the more other people expect you to achieve. Every year, it all begins all over again.
- Mental health through mindfulness and study is vital; you cannot lead unless you are fit to lead.
- Don't let self-consciousness get in the way of connecting with your people.

CHAPTER 12:
THE BEST IN THE WORLD FOR THE FUTURE

MAKE SURE YOUR BOARD MEETINGS DON'T TURN INTO BORED MEETINGS

According to Porter's Five Forces, a trusted model for analysing the competitiveness of a business, DHL is extremely well positioned for the future. The forces are as follows:

1. **Competitive rivalry**. This refers to the number and strength of your competitors.
2. **Supplier power**. This is determined by how easy it is for your suppliers to increase their prices.
3. **Buyer power**. This is determined by how easy it is for buyers to drive your prices down.
4. **Threat of substitution**. This refers to the likelihood of your customers finding a different way of doing what you do.
5. **Threat of new entry**. This is the ease with which other companies can enter your market and compete with you.

There isn't a lot of competition in our industry: between FedEx, UPS and DHL, we have between 70 and 80 per cent of the global market. It's not just the capital expenditure that is involved or the infrastructure that needs to be set up in every country – it's also the experience over many years with many different cultures that has allowed us to build up this kind of network. I can see Amazon competing against us in virtually any domestic market in the world, but I can't quite see them having the capability to build a global network that would compete with ours.

And even if you build global networks by acquisition, it's difficult to put them all together and make a cohesive system – this is something that our competitors are finding out, to their cost. The international express business is a very difficult beast; it's difficult to be truly global, so the threat of substitution and new entry is lower than in many other industries.

I am realistically optimistic about the future, because the growth of the marketplace seems robust, and almost all businesses seem to be growing. I think it's important to mention the need to capitalise on the e-commerce revolution, and can see two primary dimensions for this. The first is online shopping by individual consumers; it's not just the marketplaces such as Amazon, Ali Baba, JD com., Rakutan and others that will continue to grow, many e-tailers and smaller marketplaces are setting up at an exponential rate and it is obvious that every single bricks-and-mortar retailer will also need an online offering. Secondly, business-to-business operations are already massively increasing their online transactions. Both these avenues of business are transacted globally and we will be able to support such growth. The e-commerce revolution requires a strong logistics operator, and as a key enabler of the digital age, we are well placed to fulfil that role. We will use technology to keep us at the forefront of the customer experience, but our overriding strategy remains simple: to specialise in the international side of our business.

THE FUTURE OF OUR BUSINESS

E-commerce has the ability to connect people, products and services in places thought impossible even just a few years ago. The developing countries of yesteryear are rapidly becoming the powerhouses of the future.

When DHL began we were a purely physical business. The need to transport paper waybills, typed invoices and suitcases full of documents gave us the means to connect businesses and help them grow. Today we are in an age of digitalisation where DHL enables the physical realisation of e-commerce. The flow of digital information is as important to our success as the flow of shipments. Global e-commerce businesses and their customers benefit from the reliability, security, speed and regularity of a service we've developed over 50 years.

If digitalisation is the way forward, data is the fuel. By collecting it, organising it, sharing it and analysing it, we provide our customers with competition-beating quality. Already, we can create new sales leads with our DiscoverDHL.com digital platform. It publishes original, relevant content that attracts the right types of audience. We offer users content that interests them in exchange for their details and this data allows us to customise our communications to suit them.

Once we have secured the customer's business, digitalisation will help us provide a level of service that has not been possible before. Using data and algorithms, we'll be able to not only track but to predict the progress of a shipment across the world and flag up when it is in danger of missing a checkpoint. Proactive data monitoring is set to revolutionise international shipping. Our systems will soon be anticipating and alerting us to issues across the network. For example, if a shipment is scheduled to arrive in Nigeria at a certain time, we will have built-in alerts along its pathway to indicate if it's on time or not.

To support the ever-increasing pace of e-commerce, data will also allow us to become even more flexible with deliveries, monitoring and reacting to last-minute changes. Combining the power of a next generation Global Courier Application and On Demand Delivery, we'll be able to send a text saying 'we'll meet you there!'. And as data-driven services such as MyDHL+ (our online shipping platform) expand, customers will not only have the clearest, simplest and easiest-to-use platforms in the express industry to book, track and pay for their shipping, they'll be able to access them in the palm of their hand, from anywhere in the world.

Digitalisation will enable us to get closer to the customer than ever before, combining their profile, preferences and history from all our systems and presenting it to our teams with greater clarity and ease. Already we have Customer 360 pulling together information from Operations, Billing, Customer Service and Sales, so for the first time we can see a full picture of every customer in one place. This is just the beginning of intelligence-driven platforms delivering an extraordinary level of information and insight across DHL. Soon we'll be able to predict the customers' future requirements before they even realise what they need.

For both multinational companies and the start-up SMEs, it's this kind of service that will keep DHL as their supplier of choice for the next 50 years. However, despite the technological advances, AI innovations and awe-inspiring leaps in computerisation, what will always make DHL unique is our dedication to picking up, delivering and service quality that only motivated, passionate people can achieve. The human touch will always offer something more than technology ever can.

The technology has to be subservient to the people who know the business inside out, because they're the people who can lay out most clearly what the business needs. The older the business, the more knowledgeable and careful one has to be about changing anything; if you already have a functional system and a satisfied customer base, you need to incrementally improve each element of the business and attract new customers while also raising the satisfaction of all your existing customers. Radical change by people who are oblivious to the consequences of their actions can imperil the core of the business.

In business, there are no shortcuts: people who try to make fundamental changes overnight can cost their investors a lot of money. And turnaround specialists who are brought in from outside a business often turn out to have a disastrous effect. This is why a great number of Fortune 500 companies disappear from the list every decade. Building a great business is a grind, and only appears glamorous and easy to those people who don't know how much hard work it really takes.

Many consultants approach me with 'asset light' or 'virtual' models, and talk to me as if e-commerce is the only kind of commerce. The truth is, that even the most successful businesses in e-commerce and asset-sharing, such as Uber and Airbnb, are based on actual assets, because they are owned and operated by actual people. When you take on the responsibility of operating assets, you have to be disciplined in your pricing and management of them. You also have to know what your service is worth and have confidence in it; if you are constantly worrying about being undercut by the next start-up, you'll fret yourself into a premature death and also risk undermining your business.

Every industry is different, and one of the things that defines the express logistics business is that success in the industry requires long-term experience. Both DHL Express and our closest competitors have management teams that have been in place for a long time. It's a game that requires process, discipline, capability and experience, in equal measure.

There are many people who want to create a model for a crowd-sourcing delivery company that would be something like Uber. However, if we believe in our strategy – that motivated people are our greatest asset – then we should realise that an outsourced model could never work as well. We have to be true to our beliefs and execute them, realising that expertise is an essential part of the mix. We are able to charge a premium because our customers trust us with their valued possessions and assets, even across international borders. No matter how automated the service appears to be, we must never forget that we're the custodians of our customers' precious packages, and the reason that they're paying us to expedite delivery is because time is of the essence. There are entire futures depending on each delivery, and there's no app that is able to take that into consideration.

IT'S NOT WHERE YOU'VE COME FROM, IT'S WHERE YOU'RE GOING THAT MATTERS MOST

I've come a long way with DHL, but the test of a leader's performance should be not what they've achieved in the past, but the foundation that they've laid for the future. And by that measure, I'm very proud of the leader that I've been. We've developed deep bench strength, and as good as our past leaders have been, I believe the current generation are our best ever: people such as Ken Lee, Mike Parra, Dom Ming Wu, Travis Cobb, Pablo Ciano, Alberto Nobis and Joe Joseph. I am aware that my successor will not want to be me. My advice has always been 'be yourself because everyone else is taken'.

No matter how humble your history, your future can be extraordinary. There are a lot of us at DHL who are from humble backgrounds – it seems like our industry attracts them. There are certain people in life who seem to have it all planned out, who know what they want from an early age and they go for it – and I'm definitely not one of those people. Although I've worked hard, I've always felt that I just did the best I could with what I had. I didn't look for my next position or promotion, and I didn't actively create a network or demonstrate my ambition. In fact, I was almost the opposite; when I was running DHL in Canada, I thought being on the global board was a waste of time, even though my boss wanted me there. However, once I was on the board, I quickly became one of its most vocal members. This proves that if you have a job to do and do it well, things will turn out well for you; in the long term, doing things well is far more effective than just saying things well.

I owe a great deal to DHL. Besides my family, the company gave me something to believe in and also showed me the power of a culture that celebrates talent, regardless of where it's from. And it immersed me in a global community that constantly delivers – in more ways than one! Most importantly, it has inspired me through daily examples of human achievement and compassion.

OUR COMMITMENT TO BEING THE WORLD AT ITS BEST IS A KEY DIFFERENTIATOR

I've discovered that all the best people in business want to make a difference and leave a legacy, in order to feel that they've invested their lives in something meaningful. We're competing for talent and for customers with the best companies in the world, and have established ourselves as a truly great place to work. I call it 'people power', and I think it's the most effective power there is.

When people are united around a cause, it permeates everything they do. And as you become more successful as a business, it becomes even more important that your people are aligned around a purpose. Once we've got the basics right, we have to look to other things to bring us together. It's especially powerful if you can get your core messages out to people in a fun way that reinforces your direction.

When people are happy at work, they are open to enriching their lives with other things. Being part of a global company at DHL, we see very clearly how people from every culture want to be part of something bigger than themselves, which makes them more interested in helping people. This has informed the legacy that I want to leave, which is simple: to help build a company that is an example of what the world could, and should, be.

However, it's very difficult to do anything if you're not making money. Because DHL has been through such a traumatic experience in the past, we have decided that we never want to go through such a time again – as a result, we want to ensure that we grow in a responsible way. We are not risk-averse, but we *are* conservative in terms of what our investments will mean for the growth of the company. It's important not to take stupid risks – especially in terms of acquisitions. And as I've mentioned already, it's difficult to integrate the incoming cultures and IT systems. It's also very difficult to understand what customers regard as the key sources of value in a company, so it's important to make sure that everything is in line before trying to grow. Once again, the hero is not the turnaround expert: it's the person who can grow a business consistently, ahead of the market, and improve the four important bottom lines.

Toughness in business means laying out what you expect and then providing people with the training, resources and guidance that will enable them to achieve it. And if people cannot do it, or choose not to, they need to move out. If a star player on a team is past his peak, he should move on for the sake of his team. I'm aware that I push people hard, but I also recognise their contributions. The key thing is creating an environment where people acknowledge any problems, but can also suggest a solution without fear of being shot down. That's why you have to spend time with the people on the front line and not just with top management. If they see you as accessible, and you're able to narrow the gap between leadership and the people who do the real work, you will be well placed to spot the real talent in your business.

PROCESS IS THE BACKBONE OF PERFORMANCE

From a process point of view, at DHL we have to ensure that the whole world responds to and enforces our global standard operating procedures. If you allow the world to manage itself, fiefdoms will spring up. You need to find the right balance between being local (which gives you the best access to customers) and being part of a global network. We need to be centralised and decentralised at the same time, which is a real balancing act, and requires a tight control over process, finance and marketing communication. But at the same time, it's important to enable leaders to have autonomy in their respective countries – we set people free to apply our global disciplines in ways that are best for their cultures.

We're acutely sensitive to the impact that every single pick up and delivery might have on the brand. The success of DHL helps bring people together, and we want to be aspirational to our customers and our employees. When we build the excellence of the brand, we also build expectations around the brand, which means that we subsequently have to be able to deliver against those expectations or risk suffering the consequences. From the way that our people act to the way we drive our vehicles – all these things affect the perception of the brand.

EXCELLENCE SPEAKS THE SAME LANGUAGE ALL OVER THE WORLD

I'm constantly amazed by the common frame of reference that exists across the 220 countries in which we operate. Of course, there are many cultural differences between the Swedes and the Singaporeans, the Americans and the Armenians, and the Irish and the Iranians. But I always notice that their differences are overshadowed by their similarities. In our global meetings, even our staff from the most reticent cultures are happy to speak up, because we have created an environment in which people can confidently share their ideas and express their points of view. In fact, it often seems that the only difference between all our people is their accents!

LEADERSHIP MUST BE VISIBLE

In order to be an effective leader, I must be able to see my people and they must be able to see me. Leaders cannot expect their employees to do things that they are not prepared to do themselves. At DHL, I've always emphasised the idea that everyone in the organisation must be an ambassador for the company and a champion for the brand. What's more, in the modern age, every moment that you spend on the front line as a leader can be multiplied by the number of selfies and videos that are taken with you. Real respect from one's people and customers isn't bought – it's earned.

My best moments at work never happen when I'm behind my desk, and one of the reasons for this is that I'm *never* behind a desk these days. I have a stand-up desk that faces a wall, which means that there's never anything between me and colleagues who want to approach me. I've also adorned my walls with icons that have become part of the DHL Express folklore, some of whom I mentioned earlier: Yoda, Maximus the gladiator, Arthur Christmas and Lady Gaga. I also have a cut-out of Jim Henson's Muppets shouting 'Sell, sell, sell', which reminds me of what I should spend every day focusing on. All these icons motivate me to be a cheerleader for every one of the 100,000 people who represent the DHL brand.

Over the years, we've built a fabulous and balanced scorecard, an example of which is included on page 186. This kind of scorecard gives us a high-level, periodical view of the elements affecting our business: the level of employee satisfaction, the transit times that influence our great service quality, market share driven by our loyal customers and the profitability of our network. We have also created a global Quality Control Centre that is fully computerised and shows me instantly if we have an issue in any area of the business. We have such a robust network and these things are so closely examined, that when something happens in a particular area, I hear about it immediately. At DHL, people realise that it's better to share problems immediately rather than sweeping them under the rug. People know that if they tell me, I won't hold it against them. Then the network can help them fix the problem.

Business is a contact sport, which means that you have to be out there in front of your customers and coaching your people. It was as a result of this thought that we came up with the metric that if you're in a management position, 70 per cent of your time should be out of the office in front of customers or motivating your people. After all, if you're not going on customer visits with your people, how are you able to know how well or badly they're doing? I have a simple rhyme I use: 'On the floor or in the field, reducing cost, improving yield'.

EVERYONE CAN TALK ABOUT THEORY, BUT IT'S THE EXECUTION THAT COUNTS

You have to believe completely in the mission of the company, and you also have to be vocal in your commitment to executing it. I mentioned Peter Drucker earlier, on how the purpose of a business is to create and retain a customer. The only way to achieve that purpose is to be out there on the ground, spending time with the customers and speaking to your employees. Leaders need to reaffirm that everything begins and ends with the customer. Our ability to grow and make money is all about their needs, and our ability to innovate comes from listening to them. As a leader, if you don't do it, no one else will – if you aren't a role model, then no one will do the right thing. If the people at the top don't follow the rules, the rules will cease to exist.

A key distinction for me is how you think and feel versus what you say and do. Even on the days when I don't feel good, it's important that my words and actions still inspire the right actions in my people. It's critical that my personal moods don't in any way dictate the quality of my leadership.

We want people who can execute, which is why I believe that having only one strategist at the top conveys a powerful message to the rest of the company: it's simple, but it's not easy. We can never believe in our own rhetoric. It's the customers' feedback that counts most of all, and when our people know that we're serious about being customer-centric, they are able to execute. We've managed to codify everything that our employees need to do. They're all recognised as Certified International Specialists, and we want them to bring their own warmth, personality and ideas to the work. Nobody who works at DHL can claim that they don't know what they need to do; they just need to do what they know.

KEY LEARNING

- The best solutions are those that cut through the clutter.
- Panic and desperation never lead to successful strategies.
- Don't be inhibited by your background – be inspired by your future.
- When we build the excellence of the brand, we also build expectations around the brand.
- If the people at the top don't follow the rules, the rules will cease to be the rules.

CHAPTER 13:
THE SIMPLICITY OF HAPPINESS

YES – IT'S MONDAY MORNING AND I'M BACK AT WORK AT DHL

A recent article in French magazine *Air & Cosmos* described me as 'the man who transforms those around him: he has the rigor of the Germans, the humour of the English, and the enthusiasm of the Americans. But who is he really? Everyone agrees that in every respect, Ken Allen is an atypical character'. I like that description, because it expresses the personal brand that I've built over the past 35 years.

In my role as a global CEO, I get to spend a lot of time with the great and the good, and I also have plenty of time and space to think. I often find my thoughts turning to the really big questions regarding the role of business in society. Again, for me it's simple – as leaders of global businesses, I think we have an obligation to make the world of work better and by doing that, we will make the whole world a better place, too. At one level – on a macro scale – the world is getting infinitely better. We have no major wars, child mortality has plunged by half in the last 30 years and life expectancy has risen by decades within a matter of decades (it has increased by 20 years since 1960). Extreme poverty has reduced dramatically and basic education, literacy rates and vaccinations have accelerated rapidly. We have every reason to be happy, and everyone deserves to be.

However, I also read far too much about employee engagement flatlining globally. Simply put, the people in our organisations are far from happy with the experiences we create for them, and that really upsets me. The attitude of our front-line people is the one most frequently seen by customers, so we need to ensure that we focus on keeping them motivated and optimistic. I have always wanted everyone to come to work saying things like, 'Yes, it's Monday morning and I'm back to work at DHL Express!' with a spring in their step. It's another simple idea, but happy employees usually mean happy customers and happy shareholders.

Happiness is a philosophy we need to take seriously, and our key goal as leaders should be to create a positive attitude in business – especially if the organisation we run is going through uncertain economic or competitive times. A few years ago I read an amazing article in the *Wall Street Journal* by the health reporter Melinda Beck, which crystallises what a positive view of life can bring.

I always challenge my leaders to ask themselves, 'Do I make people happy when I walk into the room or when I leave the room?' And when things go wrong, either personally or professionally, I always try to encourage them not to say 'Why me?' but rather 'Why not me? And how do I fix it, learn from it and carry on?' At DHL Express, we are constantly looking to motivate our people to make sure they work in a supportive environment that drives them to make the customer happy. Loyal customers are, in fact, the only guarantee of success and growth that we have. And to do this, everyone in a management or supervisory position needs to walk the talk.

Another simple truth about happiness is that it's not wise to expend energy focusing on things that are not within your control. In business and in life, things will come along that create uncertainty and possibly threats. When they do, look them in the eye, embrace them and find ways to co-exist positively with them. This is no more true than the time I see spent worrying about emerging technology, digitalisation and tech disruptors in every industry. My view is 'Don't worry – be happy!' Technological advancements such as digitalisation, robotics, AI and the Internet are things that are inevitable, and the reality is all this new technology actually makes our life simpler. It is far easier to keep in touch with friends and family, to choose music or films, book a flight or a room, or find any kind of information you want on health, insurance, fashion or virtually anything than it ever was. I am also not at all worried that someone will disrupt our business. Because of our connections and business intelligence, we're able to constantly scan the horizon for disruptors. We're always talking to customers, and we're not playing someone else's game – we're playing the game that we are experienced at and that we know works well. And, what's more, we're getting better at it every day.

The principle is not to worry about the speed of this change – if you focus on doing the right things in the right way, you'll be at forefront of change. The business problem and opportunities should come first – then you have to find the technology to help you solve them. Technology is an accelerator, and it has to be used for the right reason. When you know where your business is going, and you know where your customers are and what they're looking for, it's inevitable that your people will be motivated to find and use the latest technologies, to rise to the challenge and invite the leadership to give them the best tools.

Creating happiness at work starts by creating happiness in our personal lives outside work. I want my family, friends, customers, employees and shareholders to be well and happy – in fact, I want that for the whole world. So how do you foster this kind of happiness? The happiest person I know is the second of my three sisters – she believes, without any doubt at all, that what she and her colleagues are doing will make the world a better place and she has an amazing, if somewhat weird, sense of humour. She also happens to be a Carmelite nun in a closed order and she has been living there for 25 years. The convent is high in the hills of the Peak District near Sheffield, and she isn't even allowed out for trips. One time when I went to see her (she sits behind a screen, like she's hearing confession), the wall around the convent had been partially demolished in a storm. I said to her, 'Hey Julia, you can escape – make a break for it!' to which she said, 'Ken, these walls are to keep you out, not to keep me in'. I admire Julia for her serenity, her belief in the good of humanity and her grounded, common-sense approach to life. She stops me from taking myself, and the challenges I face every day, too seriously. I'm also lucky that the rest of my family keep me grounded, too. My dad constantly asks me, 'What do you really do all day?' or 'What do you do in China? You can't even speak Chinese!' or 'Why do you visit all these fancy places – don't you trust your managers?' And of course, none of these questions are easy to answer to his satisfaction.

For me, this is part of the key to happiness – it's important to stay grounded, try to see the wood for the trees, don't worry about what you can't control – and never, ever take yourself too seriously. Also, always remember to be yourself. What I mean by this is that we should all try to find an organisation with a culture that roughly fits with us. Don't try and change the culture, because not even CEOs can do that – all they can do is emphasise and build on the positive elements of what is already there, which is generally the reason they joined the organisation to start with.

I think doing what you love and doing it the very best that you can is central to happiness. It's a philosophy I take across all elements of my life – and it pays off in making me the leader and CEO I am. My CEO of Asia, Ken Lee, worked on this fabulous framework that came out of my principles of SELF Reflection:

More empowerment. Less bureaucracy.

Support. Not direct.

Enable. Not regulate.

Add value. Not more work.

Trust and train your people.

Celebrate success, have a good time and be happy. Happiness is the ultimate destination.

The reason I'm always finding breakthroughs is because I'm always looking for them. I don't ever get complacent. I don't ever mistreat people. I'm never in cruise mode. I'm always curious. I know there is always a way, especially when others say that there isn't. And most importantly, I'm always grateful.

I believe that in order to sustain an attitude of gratitude and happiness, it's important to know the aspects of your life that are most important to your well-being and take as much care of them as you can. The four aspects of my life that are most important to me are my health, my family, my work and my friends.

MY HEALTH

I don't want to live forever – I just want to be healthy when I die, and to be able to do as much as I can, for as long as I can. I accept that there are things that I'm not able to do at 63 that I could do at 33. I also realise that there are some things I won't be able to do at 83 that I can do now. All these things are ok though – all I can do for the moment is take as much care as possible of my physical and mental well-being.

I try to work out six days a week. I also eat healthily, especially when travelling, and I take vitamin supplements to enhance key functions. I drink very moderately. I get enough sleep. I stay hydrated, especially on airplanes. I read both fiction and non-fiction. I meditate. I listen to great music. I give myself regular breaks and visit rejuvenating places.

MY FAMILY

My mother and father built an incredibly strong unit that stayed together through life's ups and downs, and instilled in me a sense of how important family is. My family means everything to me – I'm only able to think of myself in the context of my wife, children, parents, in-laws and siblings. I am blessed by each one of them. I love my mother-in-law and brother-in-law like my own family and their well-being is as important as my own. We're always delighted to see each other, and when we get together, it's a fantastic celebration. The older we get, the more we seem to savour each other's company.

It's true that behind every successful man is a woman who gives him permission to succeed. I see my wife, Gigi, as an extension of myself. I met her through work in early 1987, and she changed my life forever – I always think that whatever else DHL has given me, Gigi was the greatest gift. She is integral to my 'inner team' – we have different responsibilities, but common goals. She provides me with honest reflection and unconditional support. I'm committed to staying with her forever, because without her I don't feel complete. I miss her when we are apart, but also give her the space to live her own life. I relish our frank dialogues about everything.

Gigi is my perfect partner. I had to travel halfway around the world to find her, but I'm so glad I did. As she says about our partnership:

Maybe our love is so strong because we are apart so often. Absence does make the heart grow fonder. We've been married for 30 years. One of the things that I did right is that I never nagged him. Even though he travels so much, I totally accept it. It's simple – if you love someone, you will do so much for that person. It makes everything work. It's also about prioritisation. I never worry him about anything unless it's important. And he will always answer my call or my text immediately. He never – ever – makes me feel like I'm bothering him with things that are more important than work. And I've created my own life. I'm very curious and I've developed a lot of interests, including in news, investments and politics. That's my advice to the spouses of CEOs: be independent, develop your own interests and don't rely on your spouse to keep you interested. You need to bring something into the relationship beyond just family.

As for my children, I agree with Khalil Gibran when he wrote:

Your children are not your children.
They are the sons and daughters of Life's longing for itself.
They come through you but not from you,
And though they are with you, yet they belong not to you.
You may give them your love but not your thoughts,
For they have their own thoughts.
You may house their bodies but not their souls,
For their souls dwell in the house of tomorrow,
Which you cannot visit, not even in your dreams.

You may strive to be like them,
But seek not to make them like you.
For life goes not backwards nor tarries with yesterday.
           Khalil Gibran, *The Prophet* (Knopf, 1923)

I believe in providing my children with the following things:

1) A safe, secure and stable base.
2) Support in their endeavours and encouragement of independence, while always being there for them.
3) A great education and unconditional love (plus a bit of financial support).

All my children are miracles to me. I'm amazed when I see who they are and what they are becoming – I'm privileged to be a part of their lives.

MY FRIENDS

Whether they are companions that you may have known for many years or just a few months, friends are people whom you find interesting and who are interested in you. They are there for you when you need them most, or when you just need some fun. In the words of Billy Joel, they love you 'Just the Way You Are'. They make you comfortable, but are also willing to make you uncomfortable should the circumstances demand it.

If I'm brutally honest with myself, I can't say I have a large circle of friends. Maybe it was being part of a large family or having to leave many of my childhood friends behind as I endeavoured to build a new life for myself away from my home town. And a career that demanded a sometimes nomadic existence doesn't always lend itself to building friendships. These are some of the sacrifices you have to make to pursue a career you love. However, that just means that you appreciate your closest friends all the more. I've made a handful of incredibly good friends over the years. They live literally all over the world, but I make an effort to keep in touch and to ensure that we see each other regularly, because otherwise the relationships just fade away. They share my values and priorities, and they enjoy the same pursuits as me. The

The shrine, my office – where the customer always comes first.

On the runway, in the office – fashion is never out of style.

Horbury, West Yorkshire – centre of the universe! © 2015 Richard Bell.

Annual Asia Cup, a great bunch
of supporters.

The Republic of DHL,
no visa required.

One off the bucket list – ringing the
closing bell on Wall Street. © 2017 NYSE Group, Inc.

A spokesperson for the international express industry, on CNN with Zain Asher. Courtesy: CNN

160 HR awards in 2018.

It's a hard life – round the world sailor, Susie Goodall and Bond girl, Jane Seymour.

Signing for 14 777s – a high point.

Our Disaster Response Team, supporting NGOs on the ground around the world.

Appreciation week in China. Even I do the cooking!

And a record 200 awards for customer service.

Allen Inc. – Danielle, Alex, Nicole, myself and Gigi.

EuroCup, game on.

The most focused team in logistics and the best dressed – Vetements of course.

Our CIM certified supervisors graduate, with honours!

Community is at the HEART of everything we do.

Me and John, the new DHL Express CEO, then and now.

older I get, the more important my friends become; great conversation with fantastic people is one of life's greatest joys, and when you have the right friends, music, sport, travel, and food and drink are all enhanced by their presence.

MY WORK

I've been working for almost half a century now, and from my very first day at the Slazenger factory in Horbury, I saw my work as a way that I could reach new worlds and opportunities. The secret of my success is that I always did my best in every job. My results spoke for themselves and led me to the next opportunity. I love my job but also know that nothing lasts forever, so I want to make the most of every day.

I'm fortunate to be rewarded handsomely for what I do, and I have been amply recognised and appreciated. I've always tried to appreciate others in turn; when I find great people, I'm keen that they are greatly compensated for their contributions. My career at DHL has been synonymous with exploration, expansion and excellence. Together with my colleagues, we are constantly helping the organisation achieve things that it has not achieved before. Solving unprecedented crises and complex problems are what I do best, so I'm more than happy for them to keep coming!

Steve Jobs summed up the ideal approach to work way better than I ever could when he said the following:

> *You've got to find what you love. And that is as true for your work as it is for your lovers. Your work is going to fill a large part of your life, and the only way to be truly satisfied is to do what you believe is great work.*

I truly love these four elements of my life – my health, family, work and friends. I take care of them, I trust them and I let them define me. My best advice for finding the happiness you need to help you be the best version of you is surround yourself with the things you love most in life, cherish them, protect them and the rest will simply flow.

CHAPTER 14:
HOW TO DELIVER A PACKAGE
A SIMPLE GUIDE

Everything in life should be as simple as possible but not simpler.
> Albert Einstein

When our customers take receipt of a parcel from DHL, they don't think much about the delivery driver whose touchscreen they just scribbled their signature on, or about the other people who made this miracle possible: the sorting centre operators, the airside workers, the customs brokers or the service centre leaders who all ensured that their delivery arrived on time. Ninety per cent of these people are unseen by the recipient, and most of them will never interact directly with a customer, but within DHL, these miracle workers have a dedication to please the customer that is completely off the scale. They are all, as we like to say, 'Insanely Customer-centric'.

These people help to ensure that 230 million shipments a year are moved without delay or damage from sender to receiver. This is the work of the Big Yellow Machine, the nickname we coined for the people, processes, vehicles and infrastructure that all work together to keep the company's global economies vibrant and our customers satisfied. To anyone outside of DHL, it might sound slightly impersonal, but to all of us who are inside the business, it's a name we use with pride.

The Big Yellow Machine celebrates the grind, the relentless handling and processing of shipments that requires 100 per cent of every employee's attention, every second of the working day. It requires a constant focus on both the package that is in front of them and the big picture that they cannot necessarily see, but always know is there. It encapsulates processes that are so globally uniform that an employee working in the sorting centre in Shanghai today could move to work in Stockholm tomorrow and still know exactly what to do. These are processes that have evolved over 50 years to achieve the maximum efficiency and productivity, but that can still evolve further whenever there is a new advance in technology or behavioural science.

The Big Yellow Machine informs the design of our buildings, equipment, conveyors and tilt systems, which are the same in over 10,000 facilities across the planet. It embraces the 35,000 couriers who pick up and deliver the packages to practically any address in the world, the 92,000 vehicles they drive, sail or pedal and the red, black and yellow uniforms they all wear.

The Big Yellow Machine also governs the Certified International Specialist training that every one of the 100,000 DHL staff receives, from those on the front-line service desk all the way up to the people in the boardroom. It also covers the hundreds of IT systems we rely on to record, transfer and analyse our data, and even the methods we use to stack the millions of individual packages in our aircraft and road trailers every day. It embraces people of every race, colour, gender and political persuasion, without judgement or prejudice. It is multilingual and multi-ethnic, and it works to ensure that customers get what they were promised – excellence, simply delivered.

To get a sense of the scale of the Big Yellow Machine, it might be useful to look at just what it takes to deliver a single package from one side of the world to the other. Let's take a typical example – a shipment sent from London to Alice Springs in the Outback of Australia. It all starts with a booking, most of which are now taken online. Our systems enable us to capture most of the data necessary to help us collect, invoice and clear the package through both the export gateway, in this example in the UK, and the import gateway, in this case in Australia.

A dispatch agent will then schedule the pick-up to the relevant courier in London who will book it into their routine – either before their day begins or after they have started their route.

When the courier arrives at the pick-up address, they identify and park in a convenient spot (the Big Yellow Machine even has detailed guidance about how the driver should park the vehicle!) and then go to meet the customer – one of around 2.8 million who use our services every year. Today all that information is contained in a state-of-the-art handset that incorporates GPS, scanner, database and a touchscreen for the customer's signature.

On arrival at the customer, our courier will inspect the shipment's packaging to make sure it is suitable and will also inspect the shipper's paperwork, to ensuring that the contents are described accurately and that the address labels correspond. If the customer is new, they will inspect the contents of the shipment before it is sealed, to ensure the veracity of the declaration form. Once the courier is satisfied everything is in order, they will scan the barcode on the label, registering the parcel as having been collected on our database. This prompts our IT systems to update the checkpoint, which means that the customer can now track the progress of their shipment online.

Our courier then returns to their van with the item, carrying it in the way they have been trained (corner to corner, incidentally). They load the shipment into the van, which has a bespoke racking system that is designed to ensure that parcels are kept secure, even in the event of a collision. When they eventually arrive back at the service centre, they unload their vehicle and assign the shipment to the correct cage for its destination. Our operations agents then load it onto a conveyor belt that leads to the outbound area – the shipment will be verified and its data is forwarded to the destination clearance team – this allows customs clearance to begin even before it has left London.

The conveyor belt then takes the shipment to the re-weigh area, where our automated technology measures and weighs it in a fraction of a second. This information is vital for both the accurate billing of the shipment and also so that our aviation team can predict the volume of packages that the aircraft will be required to carry that night. It's at this point that the shipment might also be screened for security by X-ray machines, which verify that the contents of a shipment are suitable for international carriage – items such as drugs and samples of human tissue obviously cannot travel alongside the millions of everyday consumer items that we transport each day. However, this is not to say that we are not able to carry them! The transit of medicines and organs are all part and parcel of the express services that we provide, but they require special handling and protocols and are transported via a separate workstream.

Next, our shipment will be sorted according to its destination and loaded onto a handling unit, which is then loaded onto a truck for its next journey, which is to the airport. The truck is then locked and sealed, and an alert is sent ahead to the airport, so the gateway operators know that it's on the way.

When the truck arrives at what we call the export gateway – for shipments leaving London, that is likely to be either Heathrow or East Midlands Airport – the gateway operations team places the shipment into a unit load device, also known as a ULD. For air transport, there are a variety of ULDs, each of which is precisely designed to fit the profile of an aircraft's fuselage, which means that every millimetre of space can be utilised. DHL use a variety of different aircraft – the type that is used in each case depends on such things as where they are flying to and the volume of cargo they are required to carry.

The ULD is then lifted via a scissor lift and rolled into the body of the aircraft. The floors of the freight aircraft are usually inset with a carpet of ball bearings that allow our airside teams to slide the pallets into position. This tough and exhausting work continues throughout the night, and in weather conditions that are sometimes appalling – on the hottest nights in sub-Saharan countries, temperatures can reach over 40 degrees, while in Arctic regions they can plummet to double-digit minus temperatures at the coldest times of year. In London, needless to say, it will probably be raining!

The central operation at DHL Network Control monitors the weight and balance inside the aircraft, which ensures that the containers are loaded securely and safely. It's worth mentioning that the captain will always be informed of any dangerous goods on board – yes, we carry dangerous goods, too! The reality of commerce is that many commodities that we consider dangerous, such as highly flammable or potentially explosive materials, are vital to the manufacture of the goods we all use every day. The lithium battery which is inside your smartphone or laptop, for instance, may be relatively safe to transport on its own, but put a number of them together in the same package and they can be dangerous. Because of this, our people are comprehensively trained in how to handle and pack them in order to ensure maximum safety.

The type of aircraft most likely to be transferring our package is a Boeing 757-200F – these planes are the workhorses of our fleet. From London, it will head east towards our European transit hub at Leipzig-Halle Airport in Germany, a relatively short hop on the journey that our package is making to the other side of the world. In express logistics, aviation represents a large part of what sets DHL apart from other providers. Many companies rely on aircraft to move their consignments between countries, but none of our competitors share the capacity, scale and rich heritage of DHL.

Once in Leipzig, our operations agents will unload the aircraft, taking the handling unit to the immense 43,000-square metre sorting warehouse, where our package is unloaded, resorted and loaded onto a 777, for its onward journey to the Hong Kong hub. This is no simple operation – our teams in Leipzig are consolidating shipments arriving from and destined for more than 120,000 DHL locations. Conveyors, tilt trays and scanners sort the hundreds of thousands of shipments and send them on to their allotted flight, where they are restacked, ready for transfer. The orchestration of this process is largely automated, but it still requires some 5,000 DHL specialists to ensure its smooth running. Throughout the night in Leipzig some 150,000 shipments, each of which is made up of many pieces, are handled every hour.

If you look at old photographs of the airport at Leipzig from 30 years ago, you will see just a small terminal and a single runway – it has changed a lot since then! Today, its vast footprint is some 2 million square metres, with two runways on which a seemingly endless stream of the world's largest cargo freighters descend and ascend with incredible precision. Over 60 aircraft are able to touch down, unload, reload and take off again in a matter of hours – it is the largest multimodal freight hub of its kind anywhere in the world.

From Leipzig, our Australia-bound package will begin the long journey south to our Central Asia Hub in Hong Kong, though even as it takes off, the shipment's data and images will be being sent on to the Australian Customs Authorities for clearance.

On Lantau Island in Hong Kong, the shipment will once again be unloaded, sorted and repacked, ready for its final flight to Australia. It's worth remembering that at every stage of its journey, our shipment is scanned and its 'checkpoint' recorded. This information is conveyed with a simple barcode scan, but it means that the shipper – and the receiver – can follow the progress of their package in real time as it moves around the earth. DHL was the first logistics company to recognise the value of laser-scanning technology, not only for its value to our own operations but in the transparency it gave the customer. 'Global Track and Trace' was a DHL Express invention that has since been adopted by reputable delivery businesses around the world.

When our shipment lands at the import gateway in Australia, its ULD is scanned and unpacked – at this point, the work of DHL's Virtual Airline is done. Every individual piece is then scanned separately, confirming its clearance through customs, before being reloaded onto another handling unit, bound for its final DHL service point. There's no further paperwork handling or information required at this point – the deliveries are good to go.

On arrival at the service centre, the unit will once again be scanned and unpacked, before its shipments are allocated to the various courier routes for delivery. The couriers store the shipments into their vehicles according to their priority, with pre-9.00am deliveries organised so that they can be distributed first. As the couriers load their vans, they scan each piece again, to record that it is with them, while they are en route to the consignee.

In a town like Alice Springs it is unlikely that they will have any problems finding the address they need, but in the megacities of the world, where new developments and road systems can spring up virtually overnight, even our GPS systems can lag behind the advances. Because of these sorts of problems, every courier stays in contact with central dispatch, who are on hand to answer any queries about addresses and can provide additional guidance should the destination prove difficult to find.

Our courier parks in the right spot, collects the package from inside their vehicle and locates the person named on the label. After a friendly greeting, a swift check to make sure that a suitable person is taking delivery of the cargo, a final scan and an electronic signature, the delivery is complete. The final scan matters because it's the guarantee that tells our customer that their shipment was delivered on time, as promised – and that we will now be forwarding the invoice. 'Another job, jobbed', as we say in Yorkshire.

This is the story of one straightforward shipment between two fairly accessible locations that required no special handling, no complex paperwork and no additional monitoring or temperature-controlled environment. There was no last-minute change of address and no update to the delivery instructions during the journey. It is simply one of a million shipments we moved on that night. It might seem mundane, but for us it's an opportunity to delight two very important people – the person who sent the parcel, and the person who received it. Along the way it would, on average, receive 23 separate scans and travel a total distance of over 9,300 miles.

Every inch of that long journey was performed according to the standards laid down by our global standard operating procedures, which ensure that every DHL team member follows an exact process in order to deliver – it's what we call 'The Perfect Shipment'. Each of their roles might seem fairly straightforward – after all, even an airline pilot who makes the same nine-hour flight four times a week follows a routine and sticks to the rules – but it's inevitable that exceptions occur, and when they do, we make sure we have protocols in place to handle them.

Of course, the occasional 'Black Swan' is always possible – one such example was the time in April 2010 when the Icelandic volcano Eyjafjallajökull erupted, closing the skies over much of Europe for nearly a week. Many of our competitors chose to wait it out, hopeful that the Atlantic winds would soon disperse the ash cloud and make it safe to fly again. However, at DHL we realised that our customers were relying on us and had within an hour pulled together a taskforce of our finest logistics brains and worked out a plan of action to transport our customers' deliveries via road and rail. Others can wait if they like, but that's not the way we like to do things at DHL.

In my time at DHL Express we have been entrusted with the transport of many unusual items. One day it might be a Venetian glass vase from the island of Murano, the next it could be life-saving tissue samples that are required for medical trials. Every day we carry an incredible variety of objects, from priceless musical instruments to seeds that need to be stored deep beneath the Arctic tundra, from Usain Bolt's running spikes to an endangered rhinoceros that needs to be returned to its home in Tanzania. However, I'm proud that we treat the millions of less extraordinary items, such as garments and machine parts, with the same level of care. We don't just think about the box – we think 'inside the box'. That simple yellow carton contains people's hopes, ambitions, livelihoods and even their happiness.

CHAPTER 15:
REFLECTIONS OF A
MATURE DISRUPTOR

I cannot give you the formula for success,
But I can give you the formula for failure.
It is 'Try to please everybody'.
    Herbert Bayard Swope

You might be wondering how the messages in this book relate to today's entrepreneurs. Are the thoughts of a senior businessman, who is into his sixties, still relevant to the go-getting, social media savvy, Silicon Valley-inspired millennials who might just be beginning their great journey into the world of enterprise? I think that they are; after all, I have worked for a business that was the world's first 'global pioneer' for more than 30 years.

Let's remember for a moment that DHL was a disruptive business. Back in 1969, there were really only three ways for a company to send a document from one country to another: you could use the national postal service, you could trust freight companies or you could deliver something to its destination yourself. Invariably, the national post offices were government-run organisations that operated with the same sense of urgency and purpose as other similar organisations – and this meant slowly! For businesses that relied on the rapid onward movement of contracts or invoices to keep their business moving and cash flowing, this could be a major drain on resources. A document sent via airmail could take weeks to reach its destination – and that's assuming that it arrived at all.

In effect, the national postal services and the freight operators had a monopoly on the international express business, which meant that the incentive to improve or to offer the customer an acceptable service was low. The three DHL founders, Adrian Dalsey, Larry Hillblom and Robert Lynn, saw the opportunity to disrupt the status quo. Admittedly, their inaugural flight was a relatively short hop between San Francisco and Honolulu rather than an international one (Hawaii having become part of America ten years earlier, in 1959), but it indicated that there was a new challenger in the market.

DHL's next 'international' destination was Guam, but the overseas express business model soon started to gain traction, as the Asian markets of Singapore and Japan saw the benefits of a dedicated courier that could be relied upon to deliver on time, and at a reasonable price. In some countries, the postal services were quick to realise the threat of the young American upstart that was muscling its way into their lucrative business, but rather than competing with DHL by improving their service quality or reducing their transit times, they brought in the lawyers and threatened to shut down the new pretender. This move proved to be a mistake, because Larry Hillblom was a qualified and gifted advocate who had powerful contacts in the legal profession. He also by then had an army of clients who had a vested interest in keeping DHL operating and a loyal team of tough-minded managers who were dedicated to delivering for them. As a result, the legal challenges didn't stand a chance – and the rest, as they say, is history.

DHL's genius was to spot that speed was highly prized by global businesses; before the arrival of the international express industry, companies were resigned to the fact that the world moved at a certain pace. However, Adrian Dalsey and Larry Hillblom (Robert Lynn had by this point left the business, incorrectly believing that it would never make money) showed the corporate world that they could grow their business simply by adding speed to the mix.

The global brands that became customers of DHL were happy to accept costs, as long as the service contributed to increasing revenues overall. International aviation was one of the key tools that enabled DHL to disrupt the slow-paced postal model. It now seems like a typical entrepreneurial move – they spotted a gap in the market and exploited it by applying radical thinking, advanced technology and a sharp focus on a target market. It's because I am always keen to see parallels with how DHL grew that I am always interested when fresh players enter a traditional industry and transform it with an innovative approach.

The London-based online luxury fashion retail platform Farfetch is a really good example of this. The company, which was started by José Neves in 2008, has become synonymous with the world's luxury fashion brands, yet it holds no stock of its own. José is a self-proclaimed fashion fan who began learning how to programme computers at the age of eight. He worked in luxury fashion and saw how the Internet was benefiting every kind of industry except his, so he brought together his two major interests and created the Farfetch platform.

Farfetch connects the buyers of high-end items such as Gucci flip-flops and Burberry handbags with sellers around the world. It might look like a fashion firm, but at its core it's a tech company. Over a thousand engineers work on the company's 'global platform for luxury', helping to ensuring that these high-value orders are sent from the most appropriate source via the most efficient route, using a powerful and constantly evolving algorithm. The source might be a small boutique that happens to have the exact item required by the customer and is best placed to get it to them quickly, even though they may be in another country – but that is the beauty of the Internet.

This is one of the reasons why e-commerce platforms have become the most powerful entrepreneurial enabler of the twenty-first century. The technology provides small businesses with the opportunity to compete on a level playing field with the big players in the industry – and connective businesses like Farfetch are thriving as the facilitators of this retail revolution. The customer can receive purchases within timescales that were previously unimaginable; the start-ups and boutique businesses can access audiences that were once closed to them; and they all rely on delivery companies like DHL to ensure the trade is executed reliably. Everyone benefits.

Another start-up business that has identified a potential opportunity in a growing market is one of my favourite stories of a small or medium-sized enterprise. Gymshark is a company that was founded by a student called Ben Francis, together with a group of his school friends in the Midlands. In the beginning, Ben bought a second-hand printing press and rented a business unit where he could design and create unique T-shirts. There was nothing particularly remarkable in that idea, and his was a similar story to that of hundreds of would-be entrepreneurs all around the world. However, Ben had two important advantages: firstly, he was an active body builder who was involved in the gym culture that in 2010 was beginning to become a mainstream phenomenon. And secondly he had a fantastic understanding of the power of social media to connect tribes – and the body-sculpting community was a very distinct and active social group.

What Ben realised was that there was a gap in the market for advanced and technical gym gear that could meet the specific demands of the active gym goer. He set about learning what it takes to design and develop sports clothing that people like him would love. He investigated the details of manufacturing techniques, materials and tensile strengths that combined to create outstanding sports apparel, and then he began manufacturing his own line of clothing that was designed specifically for the body fitness elite.

Ben's masterstroke was to promote his new line of sportswear not through expensive advertising campaigns or product launches, but simply by persuading his friends and fellow athletes to wear the clothes while they were working out and then to photograph themselves and share the results on social media. It seems clear that Gymshark's success is testament to the power of social media – the ability to photograph, comment and share content, and all in real time, helped spread the word about Ben's products and created an opportunity for huge growth, especially in a community as close-knit and dedicated as body builders.

Sales in Gymshark rocketed for the first few years following its launch but then plateaued, a pattern that I've seen frequently in similar small businesses.

The issue was a simple one: Gymshark had reached saturation point within its domestic market but without an experienced partner was unable to venture into the international market – Ben just didn't have the knowledge or expertise, so he came to DHL to ask our advice. We sat down with him and worked out a plan that would enable him to continue to grow his business in the UK while also finding an audience around the world. Within a year, the number of orders increased from 17,000 to 30,000 a year. The fact that international delivery came with an additional cost also increased his average basket value from £41 to £70, a result of customers ordering more to make the cost of delivery viable when they are obliged to pay a premium for delivery.

To me, the story of Gymshark is yet another classic example of the mindset of the entrepreneur. In Ben's case, it was how a young business person combined his personal knowledge of sport and social media to develop a business model that took him towards his dreams. For José Neves, it was combining his passion for fashion and computing skills to develop a platform that made the world of luxury apparel accessible to a wider audience.

For DHL, international e-commerce has provided huge opportunities for growth. For the typical customer, overseas delivery may seem like an everyday occurrence in today's globalised world, but the reality is that for everything they buy that comes from abroad, there are a vast number of customs authorities to satisfy, national tariffs to pay, and import and export regulations to negotiate. The goods may appear as if by magic, but behind the scenes a number of highly skilled and experienced specialists – from customs brokers to airline pilots – are making sure their purchase arrives as expected.

The other big benefit of data is that it allows us to become even more flexible with our deliveries. We can monitor and react to last-minute changes using applications like our On Demand Delivery service – this means that if, for instance, a customer has to go into work when they were expecting to be at home, we can reroute a package and even send a text telling the customer that the delivery address has been changed. The use of data means that our customers can track their shipments and pay for delivery on their smartphones, regardless of where in the world they are.

The great advantage of digitalisation is that it transcends borders and nationalities. Numbers are universal, so we are able to use the power of data to enhance services in every country on earth. Despite this, there will always be physical and geographical factors that we have to contend with – for instance, Africa is a vast region with a largely untapped customer base and a middle-class population that is growing rapidly. I find the way we talk about 'emerging regions' patronising – especially as the change from emerging to dominant can occur within a generation. I can recall the potential of the Chinese economy being suggested in a purely theoretical sense as recently as the 1990s; within 25 years they have become, by a number of metrics, the world's most powerful economy.

Just as China has experienced a huge resurgence, Africa could become the world's next great superpower. The average e-commerce user there is just 19 years old – they are urban, tech-savvy, connected to the world via their smartphones and keen to own quality goods. Fashion, beauty products and groceries are all popular categories among such consumers – and services available online such as booking hotel rooms and flights are rapidly increasing in popularity. Africa's increasing prosperity, inward investment and Internet connectivity further support the idea that we can no longer view the world through the lens of historical nationality. We are a global family of nearly seven billion individuals connected by technology like never before and we share a willingness to work together for universal prosperity.

All this means that for today's entrepreneurs, there's no dividing line between the domestic market and international markets – they are one and the same thing. The entrepreneurs of tomorrow must see how their vision could improve the situation for their customers and what good it could do for the world. As an entrepreneur, your business enables change, but along the way it will evolve as advances in technology, markets or social trends move on. But the reason why you started your business originally and what you and your company stand for, is the only brand identity that truly matters.

How can the lessons and experiences that I've learned operating the world's most international company be applied to a new business venture? As you would expect, I'd suggest looking to simplicity for the answer – let's return to SELF Reflection and consider a number of the ideas that I've already outlined. And as a way to think about building a business, reflection is always a good place to start.

REFLECTION

What is the fundamental purpose of your business? This is what I mean when I talk about your business's 'core'. For DHL, it was the ability to transport documents and goods across national boundaries in the shortest time possible. The core of your business should be simple to articulate – when we lost sight of our true purpose, which happened when we tried to compete for the domestic market in the US, we suffered the consequences.

My advice would be to take the time to reflect on what you want your business to be, what will make it unique and what value it will offer to its customers. We've established that, in general, a business has to make money before it can do anything else, and that its purpose is to attract and retain customers. But what do you *know* you can be successful doing – not just believe, but know in your heart you can make work. Without that, how will you inspire the people who work with you? How will you develop a coherent culture? And how will you steer a consistent course in the face of fluctuating market conditions and economic crises? Your business is built for a reason, which should be strong enough to support you and your people, whatever obstacles are put in your way.

SIMPLICITY

Once you understand the core of your business, think about the simple strategy that will enable you to fulfil it. How can your business be the best in its field and one that is going to keep growing – preferably rapidly?

It's important to stay focused on what you need to do and to disregard anything that distracts you. Identify and stick to a few key priorities – I've found that strategies with 10 or 20 points never translate to the front line successfully. Establishing your enterprise will be about making fact-based decisions – not ones dictated by spreadsheets, because anything can be made to look good on paper. Make sure you understand how what you're offering differentiates you in the marketplace, what your unique strengths and advantages are and what is the simplest, most straightforward strategy you can formulate to make your vision a reality.

EXECUTION

Execution isn't just about doing the right things – it's about doing them better, faster, more productively and more often than your competitors. But you can't do this alone, so you should surround yourself with the right people and work out how to incrementally improve each element of the business. If cash flow is an issue, the best way to solve the problem is to go and talk to your customers, in order that they can shape the brand and have a reason to believe in you. It can be difficult to understand what they truly value in your business without that face-to-face contact – and business is, above all, a contact sport.

Don't worry about your competitors, worry about your customers. You will need to bring in new ones while striving to retain the existing ones, so make sure you regularly monitor how you are performing against the following four bottom lines:

1. **The financial bottom line.** You might be doing all the right things, but profitability can still lag.
2. **The customer bottom line.** The hard measure of customer satisfaction is market share.
3. **The employer bottom line.** Are your priorities translating to the front line?
4. **The social bottom line.** Are you managing to achieve anything for the wider good?

I'd also suggest taking the lesson that I learned in Canada; solutions don't have to be perfect – they just need to be accepted by everyone.

LEADERSHIP

Everything starts with motivated people. If 90 per cent of strategy is execution, then 90 per cent of execution is to do with people. Talk to them about things exactly as they are, making sure you share good and bad news in real time – if the person who leads the business can't be relied upon to talk straight, then no one else in the business can be! Encourage your people to share problems immediately, and don't hold it against them when things go wrong. Mistakes are not necessarily failures; they are an opportunity to learn from, in order to do things better next time! And as we saw with the turn-around I achieved in the US, when people understand why things need to happen, then they will work with you on how to achieve them.

It's important that you invest in your people – not just in the training they need to do their job, but in the skills that will improve their quality of life. Expect great things from them and give them the freedom to deliver them, and they will meet your expectations. Commit to them and communicate with them – don't let self-consciousness get in the way of connecting with your employees because they are your brand ambassadors, and the success or failure of your business rests with them.

FOCUS

When you start a business, everything is a risk, but as you reach a more stable footing and achieve a degree of success you may start to lose your appetite for risk, and this is when your judgement will be tested. Is it time to innovate or time to resist innovation? The tendency will be to become more desk-bound and tied up in the figures, but while the numbers are important, they can't be your only indicator of success. Do what's right for your future, not simply what's consistent with your past. If you are doing the right things in the right way for the right reasons, the answers should be obvious.

Opportunities will present themselves every day – remember that in business you're more likely to fail as a result of having too many initiatives than too few, so the importance of focus is knowing what to disregard. Everyone will want to be part of your success story and to help you by getting involved in your business. Consultants may well offer complicated advice that obscures the blindingly obvious – as we know, no one wants to pay for simple advice. As an advocate of keeping things simple, my advice would be to stay true to your business principles – the best solutions tend to cut through the clutter.

As the founder of a business, you have the honour of defining its culture – creating something tangible that others can believe in – whether they are your employees or your customers. As an entrepreneur, you are in a position of responsibility – the culture of your business will, in many ways, be a reflection of your values

For any new enterprise, there is a very fine line between success and failure. Today's entrepreneurs are better educated, more connected and often have more qualifications than many of the great business leaders of the past. Creating and running a business requires a combination of abilities, many of which cannot simply be taught but have to be learned through experience, and sometimes failure. I think resilience, the strength to get back up when you've been knocked down or to keep going when it would be easier to give up, is the greatest attribute any entrepreneur can be blessed with. It's not an easy journey, but no journey worth taking is.

CHAPTER 16:
A SIMPLE FINALE

You can judge a book by its cover.
Thank you for buying mine.
Ken Allen

Over the past 35 years, as I hope I have clearly demonstrated in this book, I have always tried to follow my heart and stay true to myself. The best things in my life have come to me when I ventured into new worlds and trusted that if I did the right things in the right way, positive results would follow. I don't ever get complacent. I don't ever mistreat my staff. I'm never in cruise mode. I always try to be curious. I know there is always a way to get things done, especially when others say there isn't. And most importantly, I'm always grateful.

Achieving such tremendous success at DHL Express was a result of a fundamental and unwavering belief in the company's mission – what it stands for and why it exists. That's what has made me able to lead and transform it so effectively, to help it become the company I always knew it could be – one that is famous for quality of service and, in business terms, for delivering unrivalled financial returns.

I'm not an exceptional man and I don't have unique skills, but I do listen, and I do care. My success comes from being ordinary, but in an extraordinary way. I spend a great deal of time with our customers and our people, listening to them and learning from them about how to transform our business. The ability of a company to transform, to grow and to make money is, first and foremost, all about meeting the needs of the customer. All the innovations that I have introduced during my time at DHL have come from listening to our customers and trying to meet their needs and solve their problems, and all my leaders know this and strive to deliver this. They are the role models of our business and they inspire our global teams to follow their example – to listen, act and resolve all the problems that are important to our customers. After all, if the people at the top don't follow the rules, the rules will cease to exist.

I've said it before, and I make no excuse for saying again – everything starts with having motivated staff, because when people are motivated, they will listen to customers. And they won't just tell you what's annoying your customers – they'll also find ways to employ cutting-edge thinking and technology to solve their problems. They should be your eyes and ears, always listening and looking for ways to improve the service you offer.

My best leadership development has come from spending time in the field. When I'm out and about, whether I'm in Beijing or London, and I can see what the driving conditions are like, I'm able to empathise with how the DHL couriers are getting around while they do their jobs. When it's snowing or pouring with rain and I can see how people are coping while offloading planes on the tarmac at Leipzig or in Cincinnati, it is truly humbling. I have huge respect for what people on the front line do, which is why I have invested so many millions in CIS over the last nine years, giving my staff the skills, knowledge and self-confidence to be 'Insanely Customer-centric'.

As I've said before, one of the biggest realisations for me has been that if I talk to someone on the front line, they'll listen to me, but if their supervisor shares the same message with them about how great our company is, it will be much more influential. Nothing motivates someone more than their immediate supervisor; they're the real reason why people join or leave a company and spending some time with them, understanding the issues they face, will be one of the best uses of your time whatever your business environment.

In every conversation with a DHL employee, I ask them the same question over and over again: 'How can we make things better – for ourselves, for our customers and for the world?'. I believe that no phrase in business is truer than 'good is the enemy of great'. A lot of people may say that they want to be great, but don't want it enough to pay the price. Great results require great effort. As Jeff Bezos, the CEO of Amazon, has often said, 'It's always Day One'. If there is something that we could be doing better, I want to find out what it is, and before the competition does. Because no matter how good we are, we can always be better.

I think the main reason I've made such a difference at DHL Express is because it's clear that I genuinely care about our people, our customers and the business in general – it's as simple as that. If you don't really feel it, you won't do it, so you need to be in an environment where you care deeply about the business and the assignments you are taking on. You need a passion for the grind, so it sharpens you up rather than grinds you down.

The message that I most want to share is that, rather than being inhibited by our background, we should be inspired by our future. No matter how humble your history might be, your future can still be extraordinary. The great thing about the modern age is that anyone, from anywhere, can achieve anything. There is a great quote that has been attributed to the nineteenth-century Irish nationalist Daniel O'Connell who, speaking about the Irish heritage of the Duke of Wellington, is believed to have said, 'Just because a man was born in a stable, it doesn't mean that he's a horse.'

A final thought that I want to leave you with, however corny it may sound, is that happiness and inner peace should always be regarded as the ultimate destination. If you've achieved them, you don't need to go looking for something else – instead, adopt an 'attitude of gratitude' for what you have received. Don't sacrifice important things for the next shiny novelty, but rather try to be aware of your mental and physical health at every stage and make sure that you look after yourself properly. In business, there is no such thing as 'enough', but in your personal life there definitely should be. I have it. I cherish it. I'm focused on it. And, when all is said and done, it's the only thing that matters. The more you simplify happiness, the happier you will be. And as I have said throughout this book, simplicity works for me, in business and in life.

AFTERWORD:
THE WORLD AT ITS BEST

At a time when some politicians seem keen to promote nationalism and protectionist policies, companies need to step up and show the world at its best. Last year I had the opportunity to attend a football tournament like no other: it wasn't the FIFA World Cup or the UEFA Champions League, tournaments that feature world-class players like Lionel Messi and Cristiano Ronaldo; it was quite the opposite, in fact. All the players were DHL Express employees from across the Middle East and Africa region, who had come together in order to compete in an internal company competition. There was a cheering crowd in attendance and there was a surprisingly high level of nimble footwork on display, especially considering that the players on the pitch were drivers and airside workers and that it was an ordinary, annual company event.

And yet the tournament wasn't ordinary at all. As I sat there, I wished that some of the world's politicians were there too: if they had come, they would have seen Saudis, Afghanis, Syrians, Egyptians, Iranians and people from many other nations all playing and celebrating together. And the people playing football were not just men: it was all the more surprising that in a region which is generally thought to have a long way to go when it comes to gender equality, there were also female teams of DHL employees competing. These included women from Iran, Egypt, Syria, Kuwait and there was even an all-women's team from Saudi Arabia – it was something that I'd never thought I would see in my lifetime.

Something I found really moving at the time were the team members from Iran, who came up to me and Charlie Dobbie and pleaded with us to keep the DHL office in Iran open. 'We love working for DHL – and our customers need us', one of them said. The reason for their pleas was that the Iranian office was at the time threatened by the imminent onset of US sanctions on the country. The situation demonstrated to me the advantage that business has over politics. Politicians have no choice but to think about the short term, because they always have to focus on their performance in the next round of elections. Global businesses like ours, on the other hand, are able to play a much longer game, because we are in it for the future, and for all the nations in the world, rather than just one.

Watching these teams of smart, enthusiastic, passionate young people competing on the football pitch also made me think about our company's culture and about the role played by company cultures in the wider world. Many thought pieces I've read about the role of leadership in business have offered theories about how corporate culture can influence employee engagement and a company's financial results, but my theory is rather more ambitious than this: it is that corporate culture can influence the world in a broader sense. Quite simply, if large companies like ours can succeed in engaging and empowering their employees in a positive way, then I am convinced that this effect will flow outwards, like the ripples in a pond, and will cause real change around the world.

Our tagline at DHL is 'Excellence. Simply Delivered', but, it's much more than just a tagline, because we actually live it. We want DHL to be the best in the world, connecting people and improving lives and, to that end, we have made significant investments to ensure that all our employees understand our core business and true purpose. Most of the 500,000-plus employees across the Deutsche Post DHL group by now have the passport that proves they have completed this company-wide training. I carry mine wherever I go, and while I've been travelling around the world, even when I've been walking around cities as a tourist, I've encountered couriers who have challenged me to show them my passport. As a proud member of the family of Certified International Specialists, I always do, and in response, they do the same – it's a bond that we all share.

As the most global company in the world, we don't pay any attention to nationality, colour, religion or sexual orientation. We are all one big family, we all carry the same passport and we are motivated by the same concerns. At the same time, we also encourage everyone to go out there and engage with the world. First and foremost that means our customers, because without our customers we would be nothing. But our staff also genuinely care about helping others, people in need and the environment, and I'm delighted to work for a company that actively encourages and supports what they do.

For example, some of my colleagues from around the world frequently volunteer to be part of our Disaster Response Teams, which help manage logistics in the aftermath of major disasters, such as the recent earthquake in Indonesia or the devastating Hurricanes Irma and Maria in the Caribbean. We have a Global Volunteer Day every year, in which 100,000 colleagues across the globe participate in one way or another, doing everything from cleaning up beaches to helping build houses in underprivileged communities. At the start of last year, we also began to reward our employees who volunteer for good causes in their spare time. At our management conference, six regional finalists from the DHL's Got Heart campaign came to tell us their stories. This included Diego, who works with young people in Costa Rica, Tran Truc, who helps children with cancer in Vietnam, and Quinto, who set up his own foundation in Uganda to help kids there who had been traumatised by war.

These were just three of the amazing people who came to tell us their humbling stories, and they represent the admirable and inspiring work done by many others in our remarkable company. They also represent the spirit of DHL, and of the kind of staff we aim to recruit; people with passion, purpose and heart, who want the best for our customers and for the wider world. As these colleagues presented their stories, many of the senior managers in attendance had a tear in their eye – I know I did! These were incredible stories of amazing human beings who had chosen to spend their free time selflessly helping others.

I have been with our company for 35 years, and I am being completely honest when I say that I think it is a fantastic example of the world at its best. Back at that football tournament, watching all those committed young men and women competing and cheering each other on, regardless of where they were from or what conflicts their nations were engaged in, I felt that we had achieved our aim: when we're at work, we *are* the world at its best. We hold similar events all around the world, and I witness that same spirit of togetherness wherever I go. At a time when some governments are becoming increasingly nationalistic, where some abdicate responsibility for the fight against the threat of climate change, and where wars are waged for territorial or ideological advantage, this seems more important than ever. And it seems clear to me that companies – especially large multinational ones like ours – have a critical role to play in society.

After all, we connect people, we improve people's lives and we believe that isolation is not a solution. And that means we must encourage stronger bonds whenever we have the opportunity – it's a win-win situation for our customers, international trade and people everywhere. We have the means to support our employees in their development and in how they engage with others. And we have the will to help tackle climate change and develop fresh ideas, innovative solutions and new initiatives that can truly make a difference at every level of society. I firmly believe that at a time when our planet is in grave danger due to environmental problems, when people suffer because of war and famine, and when protectionism is on the rise, we all have a responsibility to do what we can.

This is not just an issue for DHL, of course – there are many other big global players who also need to step up to the challenge, and if we all make the effort, I know we can make a big difference and achieve great things. Because as simple as it may sound, each of us has the capacity to move the world forward, and together we can make it a better place. I think Mother Teresa might have said it best, when she said, 'I alone cannot change the world. But I can cast a stone across the water and create many ripples'. It is because of the positive impact that our employees have on the planet that I truly believe that 'DHL is not only the best in the world, but the world at its best'.

APPENDIX 1:
A 50-YEAR TIMELINE OF DHL

In 2019 DHL Express turned 50: this is a major milestone and as a result represents a good time to reflect on what it means to be a mature disruptor, as well as how the company got there. We constantly hear about disruptors in business, but we don't always realise that DHL Express has an entrepreneurial background, too. Founded in San Francisco in 1969 by three entrepreneurs, it gave birth to the global express industry and has grown rapidly since then, but it has also fought global postal monopolies, been on the verge of bankruptcy, been acquired by the German Post Office and, despite not making any money until the last decade, it has become a massive global brand name.

The following timeline tells the history of this great company:

1969 – DHL is founded in San Francisco by Adrian Dalsey, Larry Hillblom and Robert Lynn. With very limited capital, the three men transfer shipping documents to Hawaii, so ships can pre-clear and save demurrage charges. It results in rapid global growth, in addition to many run-ins with postal authorities. The founders' philosophy is that they each have a suitcase and a credit card, and are happy to travel anywhere they are asked to by customers.

1970 – Lynn leaves the partnership and onboard couriers are introduced.

1971 – The first DHL office opens in Honolulu and the Philippines is the first international destination.

1972 – The company expands its services into Japan, Singapore and Australasia.

1973 – DHL has its first run-in with the postal authorities in Hong Kong, as the territory's Postmaster General challenges the company's right to do business there. Meanwhile, there's further expansion into the Malaysia and Indonesia.

1974 – Operations begin in the UK.

1975 – Operations begin in Amsterdam and Paris.

1976 – Operations began in Mexico, Scotland, Bahrain and Saudi Arabia.

1977 – The parcel product is introduced, which causes another massive growth spurt. The rapid international expansion continues, as we open offices in Germany, Korea, Nigeria, South Africa, Argentina, Turkey and Eastern Europe. In total by this point, we are operating in 24 countries. Starts an airline in the US, Air Polynesia. Opening in China and India.

1978 – Operations opened in Brazil, Venezuela and Colombia.

1979 – Ten years old. Aircraft are introduced into the Middle East region and the DHL 1,000-word processor was introduced.

1980 – DHL undergoes major restructuring, to ensure it is fit for international growth.

1981 – US operations doubled in size, with the push into domestic delivery.

1983 – First Boeing 727 aircraft added to the US fleet.

1984 – DHL opens in Russia. The BRIC countries are all operating now.

1985 – It is still failing to make any money, but it is building a recognised brand; by now, the company is operating in 142 countries and territories. Major hub for Europe opens in Brussels.

1986 – 'Ain't No Mountain High Enough' TV campaign makes its first appearance.

1987 – Margaret Thatcher opens the DHL hub at Heathrow and famously declares that DHL is the 'best in the world'.

1989 – The company is 20 years old, operating in three super regions, and introduces 'EasyShip' a Customer Integrated Shipping System.

1990 – UPS makes an approach to take over the company, but it doesn't come to anything. 'Professional' management is brought in from the outside, but this results in fiefdoms in different parts of the business, with no global network culture at senior management level. Despite this, the rank-and-file and middle management are dedicated and entrepreneurially driven. By now, the company is operating in 174 countries and territories.

1992 – The company forms a joint venture with Lufthansa, Japan Airlines and Nissho Iwai; though all sides try hard, it is eventually called off. DHL is now operating in 193 countries and territories.

1995 – Larry Hillblom, DHL's creator and the company's driving force, dies in a plane crash in the Western Pacific. His body is never found, which adds to the mystique surrounding his life. He was only 52, but his simple idea had revolutionised the way the world does business. Also in this year, we open offices in Mauritius and Moldova, bringing the total number of countries to 218.

1997 – DHL introduces a global intranet to improve global communications and link all the company's employees worldwide.

1999 – Now 30 years old, the company is operating in 227 countries and territories globally. Invests €1 billion in 44 Boeing 757 aircraft in Europe. DHL highlights in its anniversary magazine 'E-commerce worth hundreds of billions every year will be driven by internet growth, prompting a huge demand for logistics services'.

2001 – Partnership begins with Northwest Airlines Cargo Inc. and DHL are elevated to the International Cargo Associated Hall of Fame.

2002 – Having been a minority shareholder Deutsche Post acquires the remaining shares of DHL Express. It was losing money and the original founders had all passed away. This, combined with a lack of capital and a need for investment, would allow the company to grow market share in the parcel business.

2003 – There is a major rebrand of traditional DHL colours to the iconic red and yellow that we see today. Sponsorship of Surf Life in Australia and New Zealand begin, incorporating the new DHL brand colours.

2004 –DHL becomes the official logistics partners for Formula 1.

2005 – The Disaster Response Team is set up and the Central Asia hub in Hong Kong is opened.

2006 – First Choice global quality system is set up.

2007 – DHL enters into aviation partnership with Aerologic.

2008 – With the global financial recession on the horizon, DHL Express records a loss of €2.2 billion. The company is almost 40 years old and struggling financially. DHL relocates the European hub from Brussels to Leipzig and moves the head office to Bonn.

2009 – DHL introduces the Focus strategy and CIS.

2010 – DHL introduces the New York helicopter service in Manhattan.

2011 – DHL launches the 'Speed of Yellow' advertising campaign, the first brand awareness activity in some years. World's first all-female crew for the Boeing 777 takes inaugural flight.

2012 – Maturity has set in: the company is disciplined, process-oriented and totally customer-focused. We make €1 billion EBIT and our market share improves. DHL opens the North Asia hub in Shanghai plus a new round-the-world flight – Hong Kong, LA, Leipzig.

2013 – DHL launches ICCC, the 'Insanely Customer-centric Culture', built off the back of First Choice.

2014 – DHL's Got Talent and the Rolling Stones Exhibition partnership are launched. Thirty years of joint venture with Sinotrans in China is celebrated.

2016 – Employee engagement is at record levels and our financial results continue to improve – we generate over €1 billion free cash flow as capital expenditures increase to almost a billion.

2017 – DHL's Got Heart kicks off along with the 'Power Up Your Potential' e-commerce campaign which leads to an additional 120,000 customers.

2018 – DHL is voted sixth in the Great Place to Work list and is recognised as a Global Top Employer for the fourth year running. Also signs deal with Boeing for 14 of their 777 aircraft, for further expansion.

2019 – DHL is 50 years old, and the ugly duckling has become a beautiful swan and the jewel in the Deutsche Post crown. Now a mature elder statesman of the business world, it is financially strong and helping the delivery of the global e-commerce boom, on time and every time.

A SUMMARY FROM DHL EXPRESS'S NEW CEO

People sometimes ask me why I call DHL 'the world at its best'. As we celebrate 50 years in business, the answer lies in our network, global presence and quality of service, delivered with passion by our people. As an organisation, we have been lucky enough to successfully expand into almost every country and territory, integrating into the local culture so that we can think global, but act local. It's this championing of cross-border trading that makes us the 'best' we can be. Now, with five decades behind us, it's time to have a look at how we got here.

A journey that started with a few men couriering documents on flights across the West Coast of America has developed into the world's most international company, employing more than 120,000 people and handling more than 230 million shipments per year, and we're still growing. Over the last 50 years we have weathered recessions, unpredictable markets and fierce competition across the world to create the international express industry as it is known today.

Today, the original vision of DHL's founders — to work with passion, a customer focus and a can-do attitude — remains. Our pioneering spirit drives us to invest in new technologies and solutions that will strengthen our infrastructure. And of course, we invest in our people.

We introduced the Certified International Specialist (CIS) programme in 2009, a programme that would both change our culture and ensure every single one of our colleagues around the world understands the important contribution that they make to our organisation. From our couriers and customer service agents, to the managers down in the hubs who oversee hundreds of flights every day, and everyone else involved in this business, the diversity of our people who bring with them a wealth of background experience and skills, is what keeps our network strong.

We have prospered with the rapid growth of digitalisation, e-commerce and global trading, especially over the past few years. Through it all, we have learned, adapted, grown and have picked up some wonderful stories along the way, many of which are included in this book.

At this pivotal point in the company's history, I have the privilege to take over the leadership of DHL Express from Ken Allen. His decade in the role saw some of DHL's greatest achievements and I will continue his work to maintain DHL as the leader of the international express industry and ensure we are ready for the challenges and opportunities to come.

As we look forward to the next 50 years, it will be DHL's team spirit that keeps us as leaders in our industry. With our commitment to continually invest in our infrastructure and people, the future certainly looks bright!

John Pearson, global CEO DHL Express

APPENDIX 2:
THE SIMPLE POWER OF PARTNERSHIPS

Another key part of the Focus 2010 strategy was the development of some high-profile partnerships. At DHL Express, we spend a lot of time thinking about how to build brand awareness and brand loyalty; every sponsorship deal we enter into is on the basis that we will have a close association with the organisation we are becoming involved in. We don't want to just pay them so we can associate with their name – we want to be their official logistics partner and build a great collaboration together, which will help to showcase to the world what we can do. Sponsorships are as important for the engagement of our own people as they are for the outside world. Employees love to see their brand at major events around the planet and it has a huge motivational effect. In my time at DHL, we have built many important relationships with brands that represent something we are passionate about or care deeply about. As John Pearson, the incoming CEO of DHL Express observes:

> Ken tends to get the best out of everyone and everything. For example, our sponsorships. The Vetements story is a case in point. We extracted every ounce of potential through the Vetements sponsorship as we have with every sponsorship from Manchester United Football Club to Stormers and Harlequins rugby teams. They've all turned into something much bigger than just the sponsorship.

Ken is a great partnership builder and also a great believer in partnerships.
They are two different things. He stays the course because he believes in loyalty,
trust and continuous learning about each other.

I have a strong partnership mindset – whether it's with a courier, an entrepreneur or a world-famous sports team, I want to create more together than we could have separately. DHL is all about enabling global commerce, and in that regard, everyone is a potential partner.

Our partnerships with iconic sports teams and tournaments are an expression of our commitment to being fit to lead, and a big part of why customers trust us as a brand. We're the official logistics partner to Manchester United, FC Bayern Munich, Formula 1 and the Rugby World Cup. In addition, we sponsor the Harlequins rugby team in England and the Stormers rugby team in South Africa. We also sponsor Rugby Canada and the Ireland Rugby Football Union. Here are some case studies that show how we work with our partners:

FORMULA E

Formula E is the world's first fully electric auto-racing series comprising racing cars that are exclusively battery powered. Working with them was a no-brainer for us. The sport combines the excitement of other motor sports with groundbreaking green credentials, so it's a great fit with our core value of speed and also supports our commitments to environmentalism. Also, as the world's first fully electric car-racing series, the FIA Formula E Championship is a pioneer and a disruptor – to me, it looks and feels a lot like a younger version of DHL Express! That's why we were so keen to be the founding partner and official logistics partner of the championship in 2014.

DHL Express is one of the founding partners of Formula E. We created
this championship together, because we believe motor sport can play a positive
role in society. Clean mobility is a key part of the fight against city pollution
and climate change. Electric cars and trucks will play a fundamental role in the

*change we need in our cities and roads around the world. When very few believed
in Formula E, DHL did. By transporting this 'travelling circus' in the most
sustainable way, DHL plays a key role in the development and growth of our
electric racing series. I remember when we first presented the Formula E car,
at the 2013 Frankfurt Motor show. Ken Allen and I were there, at the birth
of something that now has become a great reality: the ABB FIA Formula E
Championship.*

Alejandro Agag, Formula E CEO

SUSIE GOODALL

At DHL we love a brave adventurer who has a dream, which is why we were
so keen to support sailor Susie Goodall, who was the only female competitor
in the 48,000-kilometre around-the-globe, non-stop, solo race, the Golden
Globe Race, in 2018. After 157 days she was laying fourth in the field against
much more experienced captains. She had covered over 30,000 kilometres
and was sailing the treachorous Southern Ocean in 60-knot winds when
her yacht, the *DHL Starlight*, was struck by a freak wave 3,200 kilometres
west of Cape Horn. Her boat was 'pitchpoled' through 180 degrees and she
was knocked unconscious before eventually managing to send out a distress
call. Susie is a great example of the pioneering spirit that we at DHL share,
and I think her exploits nonetheless demonstrate what you can achieve if
you put your mind to it, create a great plan and see your goals as short and
achievable sprints. When you run a global brand with so many moving parts
and are committed to delivering excellence, you need to view the world in a
similar way!

MANCHESTER UNITED

DHL Express is a major globally recognised brand, so it makes perfect sense
that we would partner with other world-famous brands, in order to promote
ourselves in markets all over the world. My early discussions with Manchester United were the start of a multi-year partnership which is building
their e-commerce presence and helping them extend digital marketing

connections to the over 659 million supporters that they have across the globe. Of these, 325 million live in the Asia Pacific region, 173 million in the Middle East and Africa, 90 million in Europe and 71 million in the Americas. Again, this is a sponsorship that is all about showcasing our expertise as well as achieving recognition by our association with such a world-renowned and popular football club.

FORMULA 1

As the official logistics partner of Formula 1 motor racing, a role that the company has held since 2004, DHL Express crisscrosses the globe during the championship, taking in five continents during nine months and enabling not only the delivery of the cars themselves but also thousands of litres of fuel and oil, as well as other essential event equipment and infrastructure. Whether it's on the track itself or on the journey from one race to the next, speed and teamwork are essential. In recognition of our close partnership, we have been able to showcase one of DHL's key attributes, speed, with the introduction of the DHL Fastest Lap and the DHL Fastest Pit Stop awards, that are given to the driver with the highest number of fastest laps and fastest pit stops during the course of a Formula 1 season.

THE RUGBY WORLD CUP

We make sure the Rugby World Cup is also in good hands as DHL is the official logistics partner yet again for the 2019 tournament taking place for the first time in Asia, in Japan. For this tournament, which takes place every four years, we make sure the event runs smoothly for players, fans, media and sponsors as 20 national teams play 48 matches over a six-week period.

SURF LIFE SAVERS

The Surf Life Saving uniform in Australia and New Zealand has been sponsored by DHL Express since its inception in 2003. It's a great example of a local sponsorship deal and has supported something that is at the very heart of Down Under beach culture. DHL's support goes further than just the uniform though – it also helps with training lifeguards and providing them with the equipment they need to save more lives on New Zealand's beaches – over the past ten years alone, the service has contributed to the rescue of over 15,000 people. Every year, DHL also sponsors the Volunteer of the Year award at the Surf Life Saving Awards of Excellence ceremony, which celebrates the commitment and dedication of the lifeguards. Local community sponsorships like this one can be found all over the world and are really important in creating customer love for the brand, as well as loyalty in local communities.

VETEMENTS

Another thrilling example of how impactful a partnership can be is our relationship with the European fashion brand Vetements. Led by Georgia-born Demna Gvasalia and his brother Guram, who have a unique notion of what is classified as fashion and have long been disrupting the fashion world with their dream of taking everyday, ordinary garments, and turning them into bold fashion statements.

It seems unlikely that a simple DHL T-shirt could ignite a bold new fashion craze, but in 2016 people went mad for the DHL T-shirts made by Vetements that portrayed our company in a completely new light. It might initially seem like a crime of fashion, but when you delve deeper into the message behind the brand and what makes this simple concept so successful, there's a really revolutionary story.

Demna grew up in Soviet Georgia, where all his friends wore the same clothes and fitted into what was, at the time, an extremely regimented society. When he entered the fashion industry, he wanted to challenge the system. In 2016, he decided to feature the DHL logo on one of their T-shirts. Where many companies would have refused, we saw an opportunity: the cool factor of this brand would give us a human angle, as well as giving our brand exposure to an unexpected audience. We allowed Vetements to use our logo and we used theirs. The T-shirt became an unlikely but sensational fashion story, generating a fantastic amount of coverage for DHL and making the international press. When I tweeted a photo of myself wearing one of their T-shirts, the photo went viral in a matter of hours.

The partnership with Vetements epitomises DHL's role in enabling global fashion and e-commerce with our logistics services. It's an especially good fit for us because we are also the official logistics partner for fashion weeks around the world. I never dreamed that my most fashionable piece of clothing would be my bright yellow-and-red DHL socks – our continuing relationship with Vetements is a thrilling example of how impactful a partnership can be.

THE ROLLING STONES

When the opportunity arose for DHL to be entrusted with the transport-ation of the Rolling Stones exhibition, it was too good to resist. We're used to doing the iconic and we loved the idea of being a roadie.

In many ways, the Rolling Stones and DHL have a lot in common (although I think they're a little better on the guitar). We both started in the sixties, an era of cultural and commercial revolution, a time of innovation, challenge and excitement – a time when the old rules no longer applied but a new can-do spirit did.

Music has also been a major influence on the DHL brand – the Motown track, 'Ain't No Mountain High Enough', perfectly embodies our ethos. And music also works for us in the same way it does for the Stones – it unifies us, brings us together, it's a language we can all share and understand.

As the presenting and official logistics partner of the Rolling Stones exhibition, we've loved taking the show on the road from London to New York, Chicago, Las Vegas, Nashville, Sydney and Tokyo. And we'll continue to support this fantastic touring exhibit, bringing the legacy of the Rolling Stones to over two million fans, as it travels to further cities around the globe over the coming years.

THE GRAND TOUR

In 2016, DHL teamed up with some of TV's biggest personalities – Jeremy Clarkson, Richard Hammond and James May for Amazon's flagship TV series *The Grand Tour*. It's fair to say we've had some fun over the course of the three seasons from the Mojave Desert, to the Arctic Circle, outer

Mongolia and every petrolhead's dream road in between. The partnership has been a fun extension to our motor-sports portfolio – it's not very often we get to name a plane 'Hair Force One'!

DELIVERING THE WORLD

As a partnership with Channel 5 in the UK, the television series *Delivering the World* was developed as we saw a perfect opportunity to enlighten a global audience about the sheer scale of DHL, from its diverse operations to its worldwide presence. This deep dive into the company's inner workings offered a behind-the-scenes perspective on what it takes to be a leader in global logistics. Along the way we met some of the incredible employees and customers that keep the business going in both built-up cities and some of the most remote places on the planet.

We sent a crew out to 19 countries around the world following fascinating stories: from urgent components delivered straight to an operating theatre for open-heart surgery, to rare seeds that are sent to safe storage unit far underground in the event of a global apocalypse.

From bomb alerts to drug enforcement agencies, the series touched on just some of the everyday hurdles that the company faces and DHL's capability to overcome everything to deliver.

The series airs in the UK, New Zealand, Australia, the Netherlands, Hungary, Slovakia and the Czech Republic.

ESL ONE SPORTS

The potential of gaming is huge. That's why in 2018 DHL became the official shipping and logistics partner for ESL One, one of the major series of ESL, which features some of the biggest tournaments on the e-sports calendar. In 2017 alone, tournaments and leagues reached over 625 million viewers.

DR1 DHL CHAMPIONS SERIES

'The Evolution of Racing', drone racing is at the cutting edge of competition – a natural fit for DHL, official logistics partner and series sponsor of

DR1 DHL Champions Series. The series takes place across the US, Germany, France, Slovenia, Croatia and even features a race around the Deutsche Post DHL global headquarters in Bonn. Drone racing is a combination of high-tech innovation and adrenaline-fuelled excitement and reaches a television audience of more than 100 million viewers.

These are just some of the major partnerships we've built over the years. We have also hooked up with many other partners and causes including:

- Andretti Autosport
- Pumas de la UNAM
- Conmebol Libertadores
- Kalitta Motorsports
- Leicester City FC
- Harlequins
- Chinese Super League
- Urawa Red Diamonds
- British and Irish Lions Tour
- Mohammed Salah
- Team O2
- Mica McNeill
- Rugby Sevens
- Maccabi Fox Tel Aviv Basketball Team
- Red Bull Air Race
- FC Bayern Munich
- Indian Super League
- FIA World Touring Car Cup and Tom Coronel
- MotoGP

APPENDIX 3:
THE SCORECARD

BALANCED SCORECARD

	Motivated People*	2008	2018
Employee Opinion Survey	Employee Engagement	63%	88%
Employee Opinion Survey	Active Leadership	60%	87%
Employee Opinion Survey	Customer Focus	72%	91%
Employee Opinion Survey	Strategy	56%	88%
	Best Place To Work (Globally)	-	6th
	External HR Awards	-	160

Great Service Quality		
Transit Time Achievement (All Faults)	94.3	96.1
Customer Service Awards	-	200
Days Sales Outstanding (Willingness To Pay)	42	35

Loyal Customers		
Market Share (TDI)	29%	38.1%
Net Promoter Score	-	32

Profitable Network		
EBIT	(€2.2bn)	€1.95bn

*Based on our annual employee opinion survey

APPENDIX 4: GLOBAL CARGO CARRIERS

TOP FIFTY CARGO CARRIERS - INT'L CARGO 2017 FREIGHT TON KILOMETERS (FTK) RANKING

By expanding our service and network, DHL Express has progressively grown into one of the world's largest international cargo airlines

1. EMIRATES
12,979 million FTKs

2. DHL EXPRESS*
12,777 million FTKs

3. CATHAYS PACIFIC GROUP*
11,633 million FTKs

4. QATAR AIRWAYS
11,156 million FTKs

5. LUFTHANSA GROUP*
10,167 million FTKs

6. AIR FRANCE-KLM*
8,582 million FTKs

7. KOREAN AIR
8,525 million FTKs

8. CARGOLUX*
8,480 million FTKs

9. FEDEX EXPRESS*
8,089 million FTKs

10. CHINA EASTERN GROUP*
6,775 million FTKs

11.UPS AIRLINES
5,894 million FTKs

During 2017, DHL Express also purchased 2,074m FTKs of capacity from other Commercial Airlines (CAL)

If the purchased capacity is added to the traffic moved on our dedicated network flights (12,777m FTKs), then we are the world's largest international cargo airline: in aggregate, **14,852FTKs**

Notes:
In the case of DHL Express, data source: BAR DWH. The figure shown is total TDI + ACS kilos moved on international dedicated network sectors (primary, secondary, and feeders); DHL FTK = Gross Load (flown kilos + tare weight) x Theoretical Optimum Distance

In the case of the other listed airlines, data source: CargoFacts.com

*entity composed of more than one airline

APPENDIX 5:
THE DREAM TEAM BESIDE ME

MIKE LIPKIN – ENVIRONICS/LIPKIN

Mike Lipkin is a superstar coach and motivator based in Toronto, Canada. He is also the founder and CEO of Environics/Lipkin, a leading research and polling company. Like DHL, he is a global citizen. He was born and raised in South Africa and lives in Canada. And he works around the world. Mike has also authored nine bestselling books on personal development and professional success; his newest – called *Dancing With Disruption* – highlights DHL as a company that is on the cutting edge of change.

Mike first started working with DHL in 2004 when I was appointed as Canadian CEO. As someone who enjoys singing and dancing in front of audiences, Mike and I immediately connected. When I moved on to become CEO EEMEA, I brought Mike in to share his message with the new region. Over the next 18 months, Mike travelled to Egypt, Nigeria, Kenya, Turkey, Kazakhstan, South Africa, Russia, Bahrain, Dubai, Croatia and Serbia. In every country, he declared the importance of 'Living Above The Line', which means always delivering above customers' expectations so they become loyal. Mike says, 'In my 25 years as a motivational speaker, this was my most exciting assignment ever. I was amazed at the energy and passion of the people wherever I went. DHL is a badge of pride for every

EEMEA employee. From Lagos to Belgrade, the only colour that mattered was yellow'.

When I became CEO USA, Mike travelled across the country with me – taking the pulse of the people and communicating the shift in strategy from domestic to international. And when I became global CEO, he worked with me to help crystallise the direction – summed up in a single word: Focus. Mike also participated in the first ever CIS training programme and is a proud CIS passport holder.

Over the past nine years, Mike has worked extensively with DHL teams around the world to help them become the best in the world – and also the world at its best. Mike says:

> *I have never worked with a company that is so committed to doing what's best for its customers and becoming the best place in the world to work. At DHL, the most important thing is growth. That means being better today than you were yesterday so you can be better tomorrow. The most valuable room in DHL is room for improvement.*

SUE STONEHAM – NKD

NKD has supported DHL Express for nearly ten years. The company came into being in 2004 when founder Sue Stoneham, working as a Transformation Director in the private equity sector, found she couldn't go to one agency to shift the thinking, change the behaviour and transform the performance of the companies under her charge. So she set up a place where commercially minded business strategists could rub shoulders with behavioural psychologists and creative thinkers – all in the pursuit of one goal – to make the world of work better. Because when people come to work and are inspired by what they do and want to go out of their way to deliver something exceptional each and every day for each and every customer, you don't need to worry about the bottom line.

When she received our brief in 2009, it posed one simple question: what would happen if 100,000 employees decided to take up the challenge of rebuilding the once 'famous for service' DHL Express brand from the inside out? Would it impact service quality, customer experience and ultimately profitable and sustainable growth?

That's what we believed. We had crafted our Focus strategy to stabilise the organisation and prepare it for long-term growth. That strategy was a simplified version of the Harvard Business School Service Profit Chain – exactly the same model Sue had built NKD around. We were a company genuinely in trouble but committed to a transformation based around people and customer experience. That was just the kind of genuine, commercial turnaround assignment Sue and her NKD team love – and excel at.

As Sue says:

> *When you start reading a brief, written by a CEO, that says 'I want my people to feel sick to their stomachs when something goes wrong for a customer', you know there is something different about the assignment. As I read through the ten pages, it was visceral, passionate, straight forward – and it stood out from the crowd. My interest was piqued from that very first sentence.*

NKD and DHL shared the same central belief: that at the very core of every human being there is a need to count, for it to matter that they show up, and that what they do today really makes a difference. But without the Herculean efforts of passionate employees, the dream of re-establishing DHL Express as an industry exemplar would remain just that – a dream. So, my challenge to Sue was to re-engage 100,000 employees in over 220 countries in under a year with one simple ambition – to become Certified International Specialists, delivering great service quality and therefore changing the financial fortunes of DHL Express.

She took up the gauntlet. The defining moment was when Sue met Charlie and I shortly after she won the pitch. As she puts it:

> *They literally 'burst' into my office, they were fired up, with enthusiasm and optimism for this project. And to this date, their belief in what their people can achieve, their passion for their customers, their visible and on-going support*

to deliver and attend programmes, to plough through countless detailed designs and help us find the golden nuggets has never failed. They not only actively and positively lead from the top, they held everyone else in the company to do the same. It's my privilege to have worked alongside them and co-create possibly the most successful company turnaround in the last 30 years!

OWEN REES – MAVERICK

As its name suggests, Maverick is a different kind of creative business – an impact agency. It seeks out brand-focused engagement, marketing and advertising projects where they can create the greatest response and return, and break new ground while building long-term strategic partnerships with their clients.

DHL Express was one of their first clients. Almost immediately Maverick developed a strong emotional connection, as CEO Owen Rees explains:

The difference that we felt working with DHL Express was immediate – they had a very strong sense of their own identity and culture, were very international in outlook and had something called the 'can-do attitude', that made them very agile in overcoming obstacles and very quick to execute.

Ken Allen joining the EMMEA region of DHL Express as CEO in 2007 was an important moment, for DHL and for our business. His focus on employees and customers was something that the people within the business very much identified with immediately, as did we. Strong communication, approachability, leadership from the front – it was a style that enabled the kind of communication and engagement of employees and customers that we felt was possible.

What followed was a series of initiatives that Maverick created or had a hand in originating over the next ten years: 'First Choice', a process improvement programme where they created a tour truck stopping off at various locations to run interactive engagement sessions; 'The International Specialists Since 1969', our communications campaign that demonstrated our international capabilities as part of the US turnaround. This led on to CIS, the immersive, multisensory programme that was inspiring, aspirational and internationally focused, supported by over 120 minutes of bespoke film content, branded and immersive pop-up classroom environments, workbooks, knowledge activities and a graduation test all created by Maverick and NKD. Within the first 24 months, more than four million pieces of artwork were designed, produced and translated into over 40 languages, as well as over 20 hours of custom-made brand training and animation that captured the hearts and minds of our global team.

Since then Maverick have continued to work with the DPDHL group of divisions on projects such as the internal engagement of the 'Connecting People, Improving Lives' brand campaign where DHL defined messaging pillars and then distilled the campaign into the key subject themes and then created a full suite of creative materials from posters to films to excite the internal audiences. It also included our 'Power Up Your Potential', a global e-commerce sales engagement programme that engaged and educated our sales force with video pitch training and a range of digital tools that revolutionised our approach to online selling.

We have been through a lot together, and I'll leave it to Owen to summarise our relationship:

> *The passion, determination, can-do attitude and support for each other that Ken and the team have showed against what has sometimes looked like impossible odds, has been something very unique to observe. That has reinforced to us that DHL is a special company, which has a natural level of engagement with what it does, and with its customers.*
>
> *We have always felt that this, together with Ken's strong leadership and now John Pearson's, their open communication style gives the business a lot of potential as the company looks ahead towards its next 50 years.*

ENDNOTES

The author and publisher have made every effort to contact and credit the copyright owners of any material that appears within and will correct any omissions in subsequent editions if notified.

Quotes

Page ix ' ... one small step for man, one giant leap for mankind ...', Neil Armstrong, *OfficialNASAFilms* (20 July, 1969), https://www.nasa.gov/mission_pages/apollo/apollo11.html

Page xiii 'DHL Express has delivered ...' Jeff Ward, A.T. Kearney, Global Management Consulting

Page 7 'Results are the only true sign of excellence'. Peter Drucker, *The Effective Executive: The Definitive Guide to Getting the Right Things Done* (Harperbusiness Essentials 2006)

Page 11 'A diamond is a chunk of coal that did well under pressure.' Henry Kissinger

Page 18 'Simple can be harder than complex: you have to work hard to get ...', Steve Jobs, *'There's Sanity Returning'* (Bloomberg 1998) (https://www.bloomberg.com/news/articles/1998–05-25/steve-jobs-theres-sanity-returning)

Page 33 'The three rules of work: out of clutter find Simplicity, From discord … ', Albert Einstein, *"The Ultimate Quotable Einstein"* (Princeton University Press' 2010 p.480)

Page 43 'Culture eats strategy for breakfast … ' Peter Drucker

Page 49 'There is a tide in the affairs of men, which taken at the flood, leads … ', William Shakespeare, *Julius Caesar,* Act 4, Scene 3

Page 59 '… take DHL to the next level, because everyone got tested in that … ', Jeff Ward, A.T. Kearney, Global Management Consulting

Page 61 'Simplicity is the most difficult thing to secure in the world … ', George Sand (1804 – 1876)

Page 62 'It is not the critic who counts; not the man who points out how the strong man stumbles … ', "The Man in the Arena." Theodore Roosevelt delivered the speech entitled *'Citizenship in a Republic'* at the Sorbonne in Paris (23 April, 1910), Theodore Roosevelt Digital Library, Dickinson State University. www.theodorerooseveltcenter.org

Page 72 'The service-profit chain establishes relationships between … ', 'Putting the Service-Profit Chain to Work', James L. Heskett, Thomas O. Jones, Gary W. Loveman, W. Earl Sasser, Jr.Leonard A. Schlesinger, *Harvard Business Review* (2008)

Page 76 '… a crisis is a terrible thing to waste … ', Paul Romer, *'A Terrible Thing to Waste'*, *New York Times* magazine (2009)

Page 84 'I have a dream', Martin Luther King, *'I Have a Dream speech by Martin Luther King.Jr'* (1963)

Page 116 'There is no greatness where there is not simplicity, goodness and … ', Leo Tolstoy, *War and Peace* (1865–1867; 1869)

Page 116 'Results are the only true sign of excellence' Peter Drucker

Page 121 'The best way to predict the future is to invent it.', Dr Alan Kay, *meeting of PARC (Palo Alto Research Center; formerly Xerox PARC*, 1971)

Page 127 'Porter's Five Forces … ', Professor Michael Porter, *'Competitive Strategy: Techniques for Analyzing Industries and Competitors'*, (1980)

Page 138 'The man who transforms those around him: he has the rigor … ', Yann Cochennec, *Air & Cosmos Magazine*

Page 143 'Your children are not your children. They are the sons and daughters … ', Khalil Gibran, *The Prophet* (1923)

Page 144 ' … just the way you are … ' Billy Joel, 'Just The Way You Are', (1977)

Page 145 'You've got to find what you love. And that is as true for your work … ', Steve Jobs, '*Stanford University Commencement address*' (12 June, 2005) (https://news.stanford.edu/2005/06/14/jobs-061505/)

Page 146 'Everything in life should be as simple as possible. But not simpler … ', Albert Einstein, attributed by Roger Sessions, 'How a "Difficult Composer Gets That Way', *New York Times* (8 January, 1950). Information from (https://quoteinvestigator.com/2011/05/13/einstein-simple/)

Page 154 'I cannot give you the formula for success, But I can give you the formula for failure; it is 'try to please everybody', Herbert Bayard Swope

Page 166 'It's always Day One', Jeff Bezos, theory based on original letter to Shareholders (1997): (http://media.corporate-ir.net/media_files/irol/97/97664/reports/Shareholderletter97.pdf)

Page 166 'Just because a man was born in a stable, it doesn't mean that he is a horse … ', Daniel O'Connell

Page 170 'I alone cannot change the world. But I can cast a stone across the water and create many ripples.' Mother Teresa

Page 178 'DHL Express is one of the founding partners of Formula E … ' Alejandro Agag

Picture Credits

Section 1

1. Author's personal collection

2. Author's personal collection

3. Courtesy of DHL

4. Courtesy of DHL and *Wirtschaftswoche* Magazie – © Handelsblatt GmbH. All rights reserved

5. Courtesy of DHL

6. Courtesy of DHL

7. Courtesy of DHL

8. Courtesy of DHL

Section 2

1. Author's personal collection, courtesy of DHL, and courtesy of Richard Bell. All rights reserved

2. Courtesy of DHL, and used with permission of NYSE Group Inc

3. Courtesy of CNN, and courtesy of DHL

4. Courtesy of DHL and the Disaster Response Team

5. Courtesy of DHL and author's personal collection

6. Courtesy of DHL

7. Courtesy of DHL

8. Author's personal collection, and courtesy of DHL

INDEX

ACKNOWLEDGEMENTS

A special thank you to Frank Appel, CEO of Deutsche Post who had the vision – and courage – to give me the role of CEO in the first place. To Mike Lipkin, who first mooted the idea of putting my thoughts into writing back in 2012. He had witnessed the transformation of the US in 2007 and at that time thought I was 'tilting at windmills'. But he stuck with me, and provided the many sensible suggestions that transformed the early drafts of the book into something resembling a manuscript. To the General Management Board of DHL Express, especially John Pearson my long term confidante and now the CEO of Express. And Charlie Dobbie, who was my 'wingman' during the US turnaround and has continued to be since. As a team, you have been responsible for the ongoing success of our extraordinary company as we celebrate 50 years of delivering excellence. Without you there would be no story to tell. To Dan McGrath, who backed this project from the very beginning and whose hard work and ceaseless efforts on my behalf with the Harvard Business Review helped establish the concept of *Radical Simplicity*. To Sue Stoneham at NKD, who picked up the baton from Mike and whose ideas helped shape and sharpen some key areas of the book. To my long-term business colleague and friend Owen Rees and the team at Maverick for endless, unyielding positivity (in the face of changing deadlines, minds and drafts), intelligent advice, practical support, organisation and proofing diligence – not to mention all the popcorn. And to Faruk

Akosman at DHL, who it's been my pleasure to work alongside for many years, for his considered input and thoughtful insights – and for helping me pull together the myriad contributions from DHL colleagues, far and wide, past and present.